Contents

Preface

Acknowledgements

1 **Introduction**   1

2 **Conceptual and Ethical Issues**   7

3 **Methods**   17

4 **Ethnic Monitoring**   57

5 **Developing Culturally Sensitive Services**   61

6 **Examples of Questions to Ask Black Patients**   81

7 **Conclusions**   87

Useful Addresses   91

References   93

OBTAINING THE VIEWS OF
BLACK USERS OF
HEALTH SERVICES

Shirley McIver

King's Fund Centre

King's Fund Centre for Health Services Development

Published by the King's Fund Centre

126 Albert Street, London NW1 7NF
Telephone: 071-267 6111

ISBN 1 85717 063 6

Distributed by
Bournemouth English Book Centre (BEBC)
PO Box 1496
Poole
Dorset
BH12 3YD

The King's Fund Centre is a service development agency which promotes
improvements in health and social care. We do this by working with people in
health and social services, in voluntary agencies, and with the users of these
services. We encourage people to try out new ideas, provide financial or
practical support to new developments, and enable experiences to be shared
through workshops, conferences, information services and publications.
Our aim is to ensure that good developments in health and social care are
widely taken up. The King's Fund Centre is part of the King's Fund.

PREFACE

This publication is the seventh in a series aimed at helping
health service staff to obtain the views of service users, and it
is written for anyone who has been given this responsibility,
whether nursing, medical, paramedical or managerial.
The series presumes no social science background and offers a
flexible approach which is very amenable to local adaptation
and interpretation.

This book in the series examines the different methods which
have been used to collect the views and experiences of health
services of black people, in order to find out how successful
they have been. Examples are provided to enable the reader to
choose the best approach to suit their own particular situation.
This section will be of use to anyone who is interested in the
subject, whether at purchaser or provider level.

The book also looks at research on black patients' views and
experiences of hospital services and details four areas which
always emerge as areas of concern: communication,
information provision, diet, and religious and cultural beliefs.
Guidance is given on how services can be improved
immediately in these areas.

This book has been produced with funding from the
Department of Health.

ACKNOWLEDGEMENTS

I would like to thank Abiola Ogunsola, a freelance research and development consultant, for her help in collecting information, providing ideas, discussing issues and letting me use her research reports. Her knowledge of the issues dealt with in the book was extremely useful.

I would also like to thank Madeleine Rooke-Ley for being more than a secretary. Not only did she type the manuscript but she also photocopied endless articles and kept an eye open for relevant material. Thanks also to the editor, Sarah Cannon.

Finally, I would like to thank those working in SHARE at the King's Fund Centre for providing contacts and abstracts of relevant articles.

1 INTRODUCTION

It has been just over ten years since the NHS Management Inquiry led by Sir Roy Griffiths recommended that the NHS should pay more attention to the experiences and perceptions of those who use its services.

The initial stimulus of the Griffiths Report has been reinforced several times – by the White Paper *Working for Patients*, by *Local Voices: The Views of Local People in Purchasing for Health*, and by the publication of the Patient's Charter – and so it is not surprising to find that there has been a considerable increase in activities directed at obtaining users' views.

The extent to which these activities are systematic and routinely cover all sections of the community is, however, open to question.

Black Populations and their Health Needs

There is a long history of black presence in the UK, yet there is plenty of evidence to show that the NHS is failing to address many of the health needs of black populations.

Data obtained during the 1991 Census suggest that there are approximately three million people of ethnic minority origin

1

residing in England and Wales, constituting six per cent of the total population.

Their residence is concentrated in urban areas, predominantly in London, the West Midlands, West Yorkshire and Greater Manchester. In some London boroughs a third of the population is of ethnic minority origin.

The geographical distribution varies between groups: Caribbeans, Africans and Bangladeshis live predominantly in the Greater London area, mostly in inner London. One third of the entire Indian community lives in outer London boroughs, with concentrations also in the West Midlands and Leicestershire. The population of Pakistani origin is concentrated in the West Midlands and West Yorkshire. The Chinese are more dispersed than other ethnic groups.

Epidemiological evidence shows that these groups are at greater risk in respect of most of the key areas identified in the government's White Paper *The Health of the Nation*. In addition, the underlying aetiology and causation of many conditions is different in these populations from that seen in the indigenous population. Very little is known about the incidence of cancer, sexually transmitted diseases, unwanted pregnancies and accidents among these populations (Balarajan and Soni Raleigh, 1993).

Little is known also about race-specific factors affecting access to health care, but those factors that have been identified as likely to affect uptake of services include:

★   Presentation of illness
★   Perceptions of health and disease
★   Encounters with services
★   Use of alternative medicines
★   Lifestyle and cultural practices
★   Socio-economic status

Obtaining the Views of Black Users of Health Services

Research has been carried out on the views and experiences of black patients, and details of how services are failing to meet their needs are provided in Chapter 5, 'Developing Culturally Sensitive Services'; but there is still a need for more research in this area.

Many health professionals are keen to learn the views of black people and to make services sensitive to their needs, but feel inadequate to the task.

The Consumer Feedback Resource at the King's Fund Centre, which offered advice and information to health professionals between 1989 and 1992, received many requests from those who wanted to find out the views of black service users but were unsure about the methods they could use.

Other writers have identified worries among health professionals that they cannot learn about the cultures of all the different population groups they care for, and are aware that they often do not know what questions to ask. Another fear is that the process of finding out could become so time-consuming as to be impractical (Baxter, 1988).

These worries are justified, but the problems are not insurmountable. The main purpose of the present book is to indicate the methods that have proved to be most useful.

Those concerned about obtaining the views of users and potential users of health services should find the information about 'Methods' in Chapter 3 useful, whatever type of health care organisation they work for: certain methods share common advantages and disadvantages, regardless of the setting in which they are used.

Those working in both purchaser and provider organisations also need to understand why there has been concern expressed about the ethics of doing research on users' views. Chapter 2, 'Conceptual and Ethical Issues', should help them not only to tackle criticism of their own work in this area, but also to ensure that they know how to critically appraise similar work carried out by others.

Chapter 4 discusses 'Ethnic Monitoring'. All those working in NHS organisations should be aware of recent Department of Health guidance on ethnic monitoring, and it is in the interest of those concerned with obtaining users' views to know how ethnic monitoring relates to their work.

Routine and systematic mechanisms for the collection of views of users and potential users of services need to be established; but there is no need to wait for this to happen before changing services in areas where information already exists.

Plenty of research has already taken place which shows the same areas for improvement emerging consistently, whatever the ethnic group or service concerned. These areas – communication, information provision, diet, and religious and cultural needs – are covered in Chapter 5, 'Developing Culturally Sensitive Services'.

Chapter 5 also examines what is meant by the phrase 'providing culturally sensitive care', and emphasis is placed on the fact that the views of black patients may be very different to those of health professionals on many issues, even with regard to what is meant by ill health and sickness.

Health professionals need to be aware that culture can influence an individual's understanding of issues and their behaviour. Knowledge is needed of ways in which economic and social structures reproduce stereotypical attitudes, racism and inequalities in health, and of how organisations can prevent individuals from putting into practice the principles of culturally sensitive care.

The development of good communication skills and of practices that help to support and supplement these skills, such as questions or reminders in nursing records and checklists, is also discussed.

Research that has already taken place on black users' views can form a basis for future research. Examples of questions to ask black patients are given in Chapter 6, as a stimulus to future work in this area.

Most of the information presented in this book will be useful to those working in both purchaser and provider organisations, but individuals within these two types of organisation have different responsibilities. Chapter 7, 'Conclusions', draws attention to the kinds of research and work with black users and potential users of services that each type of organisation should be engaged in.

It is to be hoped that in the very near future the views of all health service users and potential users, including those from black groups, will be given equal weight to the views of health professionals in all areas that affect them; and the information contained in this book is directed towards that aim.

2 CONCEPTUAL AND ETHICAL ISSUES

As the number of 'patient satisfaction' studies being carried out by health professionals and researchers has increased, so too has the amount of criticism directed at these studies. Much of this criticism is justified and needs to be addressed so that research on users' views can be carried out in a valid and ethically sound manner.

Scope of Research

One area of criticism, directed at problems with the concept of 'patient satisfaction', has been present for many years. Locker and Dunt (1978) were calling for a clearer understanding of the term 'satisfaction' 15 years ago, yet little progress has been made in this area since that time.

More recently, a health researcher at the Outcomes Clearing House, Leeds University, commented that patient satisfaction information is difficult to interpret because it is based upon the differences between patients' expectations of services and their perceived experiences, yet these expectations are 'complex, shifting and massively under-researched' (Dixon, 1993).

Comments such as these can be used to undermine the value of the user's view and decry the importance of this kind of research. It is true that 'satisfaction' is a difficult concept to work with – but is this what research on users' views is really about? Surely there are a range of issues about which it is important to discover users' views?

In relation to outcomes, for example, patients need to have the opportunity to say whether the treatment they received has done them any good. Do they feel better? Are there side effects of their treatment which are affecting their well being? If improvements of different kinds have occurred, which are the most important from the patient's view point?

Use of the term 'patient satisfaction' can lead to issues that are of legitimate concern to the patient being overlooked, with patients being confined to giving opinions about selected aspects of the care process, usually hotel services and staff attitudes.

These are important, but so too are their views on nitty-gritty aspects of their treatment and care, such as whether they consider it to have been appropriate, whether it was given in a skilled and efficient manner, and whether they were allowed to have some say in it.

There is nothing esoteric about listening to the views of different types of people. If the views of users and potential users of health services are given the same weight as the views of health professionals and managers there is no 'special problem' of patients' expectations to be addressed, because everyone has expectations.

It is better to approach this area of enquiry from the broader perspective of social science research than to think narrowly in terms of 'patient satisfaction'. Within this broader perspective it is legitimate to consider the user's view in any area.

Recent government reforms have made it possible for users and potential users of health services to give their views on issues beyond their immediate treatment and care, such as what services should be purchased on their behalf and how these services should be delivered.

The NHS is a public service and should be accountable to the public it serves. Involving people from local communities in different aspects of service planning, purchasing and provision is one way of achieving this. Their input can also play a useful part in decisions about what kind of research is important.

Ethical Considerations

A second criticism about research on users' views is that there is now too much of it and most is not being properly screened to make sure it is ethical. Pollock and Pfeffer write:

> *Despite the current enthusiasm of the NHS Management Executive for using and disseminating 'good practice' in listening to local voices, its guidelines are void of ethical considerations ...*

(Pollock and Pfeffer, 1993, p. 27)

Screening Procedures

Anyone in the NHS who has consumer feedback responsibilities will be familiar with uncertainty about whether or not research on patients' views should be reviewed by the Local Research Ethics Committee. As Pollock and Pfeffer point out, there is no agreement about whether ethics committees should review this sort of work, and practice varies widely.

These issues must be faced head-on rather than avoided. Research on users' views should be a regular practice, and this means (a) that co-ordination should take place so that the same patients and carers are not being bombarded with questions, and (b) that mechanisms should be established for checking research proposals for methodological appropriateness and for ethical correctness.

The Local Research Ethics Committee may have a role to play, but could find themselves swamped with work if they have to review all proposals for research on patients' views. A more efficient solution might be for each organisation to have a research and audit group with responsibility for:

★ Co-ordinating research to prevent overlapping of activities, bombardment of patients and reinvention of the wheel.

★ Screening research to check for methodological rigour.

★ Acting as an initial check on ethical correctness (perhaps following guidelines such as those developed by the Market Research Society). Research considered borderline could be passed on to the Local Research Ethics Committee for further review.

Conceptual Problems

One of the ways in which research on users' views can be ethically unsound is in the use of poor and inaccurate definitions and conceptualisation. Where research on black people is concerned, there are a number of ways in which it is possible to make mistakes.

'Cultural Pluralism'

First, many people feel that the best way to view black and minority ethnic people is to consider them as 'culturally different'. This approach, termed 'cultural pluralism', has been identified as the dominant one in the NHS (Pearson, 1983).

There is nothing wrong with this approach in principle, but in practice it often results in racist ways of studying black people because majority and minority 'cultural groups' do not meet as equals.

One of the ways racism can develop from this position is if the word 'difference' comes to mean 'deviant' – that is, if ethnic practices are defined in relationship to white practices which are seen as 'normal'.

Several examples of how this has occurred in the field of health education – in the Ricketts Campaign, the Asian Mother and Baby Campaign, and play and child development – are given by Pearson (1986). One of the most widespread is the belief that ethnic diets cause health problems:

> *It is automatically assumed that dietary deficiencies are* inherently *part of pathogenic 'Asian' or Rastafarian vegan diets, and are the causes of iron-deficiency anaemia and other nutritional deficiencies, including rickets and osteomalacia. The constraints of poverty on choice of available foods is rarely mentioned.*

> (Pearson, 1986, p. 51)

What is also happening in the example given above is the more general phenomenon of cultural factors being used as an explanation for differences in health. It is always unwise to assume causal connections between variables (such as religious practice, beliefs, diet etc) and health unless research clearly shows that one causes the other. The two factors may be related to a third causal factor (eg economic position).

An approach which concentrates on culture may also hold individuals responsible for practices and so adopt a 'victim blaming' position. This is not confined to research on ethnic groups and has been present generally in health promotion campaigns (Pearson, 1986). However, it is reinforced in the field of race and health because the tendency has been to concentrate on diseases which affect particular groups, such as tuberculosis or the haemoglobinopathies. Sheldon and Parker (1991) describe the problem concisely:

> *By concentrating on diseases which affect particular groups there is the risk of placing the blame on the individual and the culture.*

(Sheldon and Parker, 1991, p. 9)

Another problem with the 'cultural pluralism' approach, where the focus of attention is 'culture', is that it can lead to the stereotyping of individuals within cultural groups. Sheldon and Parker (1991) advise against taking cultural guides like Qureshi's *Transcultural Medicine* (1989) too literally. Describing it as a 'hitch hiker's guide to a range of cultures', the authors comment:

> *This is no more than a mosaic of assertions, prejudices, fragmentary facts and cultural stereotypes.*

(p. 11)

The way out of these traps stemming from 'cultural pluralism' is to recognise that society is made up of different levels, of which culture is only one. The economic, social and political levels are also important. Variables such as housing, environment, income, workplace and job status, social and family networks and social status also affect health.

Not only that, but society is not static. Cultural summaries can only provide a very general picture, which does not take account of the dynamic and contradictory nature of life. As Atkin (1991) writes:

> *Black people need to reconcile two or more cultural backgrounds. Cultural ties with their place of origin may still be strong yet they become faced with situations where they have to accommodate Western ways and values.*

(Atkin, 1991, p. 161)

Also, a 'cultural difference' approach must include 'white' culture. There are variations within 'white' culture as well as black, and practices are not automatically right because they are 'taken for granted' – by white or black people.

Marginalisation

A second issue related to research on black and minority ethnic people is that because of the focus on their 'special needs', the research is developed separately from the mainstream. This means that work on health and race is often short term, consisting of one-off projects, leaving workers feeling isolated and marginalised. It also means that very often little is changed as a result of the research.

The way out of this dilemma is more complex than it appears because it is not just a question of developing research on black people as a mainstream activity. This would be a large step in the right direction and the NHS reforms present many opportunities. Providing support and networking opportunities for workers in this area would also strengthen the research base, so developments like SHARE (see 'Useful Addresses') are particularly valuable.

One of the most difficult problems, however, is that it is not a simple matter to use research on users' views to inform service development and change. Research on consumer feedback in the NHS following the Griffiths Report found that many health authorities had difficulty implementing the results of consumer surveys (Carr-Hill, McIver and Dixon, 1989). Guidance is given in McIver (1991), but this is an area which requires considerable attention from senior management.

Voluntary Sector Support

A third issue relating to research on black and minority ethnic people is that many voluntary organisations are not able to provide either information about health needs or support for these sections of the community because the mainstream voluntary sector faces the same limitations of ethnocentricity as the NHS.

The Health and Race Project (1990) survey of 70 voluntary organisations in Liverpool found that in an area with large black communities, 98 per cent of management committees were white, 99 per cent of users were white, 98 per cent of employees were white and 99 per cent of volunteers were white.

Black voluntary organisations face difficulties in being relatively newly established, controlling limited resources, and having unrealistic expectations placed upon them by the statutory sector (Atkin, 1991).

One result is that black people often miss out on the support and self-help groups available to whites. There is a growing acceptance by health care professionals of the importance of self-help groups in supporting and empowering patients and relatives, particularly those with chronic or life threatening illnesses, such as cancer (eg Speigal, Bloom and Yalom, 1981; Bradburn et al, 1992).

Racism

The last, and probably the most important issue relating to research on black and minority ethnic people is that of racism and discrimination – that is, 'a belief in the superiority of a particular race' (the Concise Oxford English Dictionary) and prejudice or discrimination against others as a result of this belief. There is plenty of evidence that racial discrimination exists in the NHS (see NAHA, 1988, for example), but this can be a difficult subject for white people to deal with. A recognition that racism exists and that it can contribute to the health problems of those it affects often generates many conflicting emotions: guilt, anxiety, impotence, frustration and the fear of causing offence or making a situation worse are common feelings.

This can result in embarrassment when health workers are expected to collect ethnic monitoring data and carry out research on black users' views. It helps to be clear about why the work is necessary; and it can also be useful to talk through the emotions at the root of the problem.

It probably also helps to realise that racism is reproduced at many levels within society, and although individuals are responsible for their own behaviour and for each act that perpetuates racism, they are not to blame for the racism that has a historical basis. Racism in the political sphere, in institutions, social structures, popular culture etc pre-exists individuals and is outside individual control. It must be tackled collectively.

As Sivanandan (1985) writes when criticising the psychological approach to racism of Race Awareness Training (RAT):

> … *Racism is not, as RAT believes, a white problem, but a problem of an exploitative white power structure; power is not something white people are born into, but that which they derive from their position in a complex race/sex/class hierarchy … Racism, strictly speaking, should be used to refer to structures and institutions with power to discriminate.*

> (Sivanandan, 1985, p. 27)

Summary

In sum, health professionals and managers, whether in purchaser or provider organisations, can improve the way they collect users' views and work towards developing more culturally sensitive services by:

★ Not assuming their own beliefs and practices are normal.

★ Not using ethnicity as an explanation or attributing causal connections between variables such as cultural practices and health status, unless this is justified by valid evidence.

★ Recognising victim blaming and cultural stereotypes.

★ Arguing for the user's view to be considered in all areas and given equal weight to that of the professional.

★ Adopting procedures to ensure research on service users is ethically sound.

★ Making sure research is linked to action to improve services.

★ Encouraging and funding the development of voluntary, self-help and support groups.

★ Accepting the existence of racism; being willing to change working practices, language and attitudes; working with others to fight institutional racism.

3 METHODS

There are a number of methods available for research involving users of health services and these have been described in earlier publications in this series (eg McIver, 1991). The intention here is not to go into detail about the methods generally available, but to look specifically at which methods have been used to get information from black people and how successful they were.

There are examples of studies using most types of method, so the reader will receive a good idea of the range of methods available, as well as how best to tailor these methods to suit black people.

Overview of Methods Available

To start with it may be useful to give a short outline of the types of method available:

Quantitative Methods

Chapter 4 looks briefly at ethnic monitoring, which has the aim of collecting statistical information, making comparisons, and answering 'how many?' questions (eg 'How many people of Indian ethnicity were inpatients during last year?' or 'How does satisfaction with pain control differ between people of white and Indian ethnicity?').

Statistical information is collected using a quantitative research method, such as structured questionnaires, forms or interview schedules, or structured observations. These can be administered at a service site, by telephone, at a community location, or at home.

The questionnaires or interview schedules allow only limited responses to questions so that the findings are easy to code and analyse with the aid of a computer. The aim is to be able to make generalisations from the information collected, so information is collected either from everyone or from a representative sample of people.

Qualitative Methods

Qualitative methods, by contrast, collect narrative information and are useful for exploring issues and answering questions asking 'why?' (eg 'Why do many nurses feel that 'Asian' patients have a low pain threshold?') (Bowler, 1993).

Examples of qualitative research methods are open-ended interviews, critical incident technique, discussion groups, some forms of observation, diaries and search conferences.

Combining Methods – An Example

Both quantitative and qualitative methods have weaknesses and it is often advisable to use them in combination. This is particularly true for the issue of 'patient satisfaction', because health care providers need to know both *how many* patients are satisfied or dissatisfied and *why*, so they can make changes to improve service quality.

So, for example, if a hospital wanted to find out whether the majority of patients were satisfied with the pain control they received in the hospital or whether some types of patient were less satisfied than others, with the aim of improving this aspect of care to any dissatisfied groups, they would need to use both qualitative and quantitative methods. One way to tackle the issue would be as follows:

I   A qualitative method to identify whether pain control was an important issue for patients or some types of patients in their hospital – although the relevant literature would probably already have indicated that this was an issue worth investigating (eg Thomas and Rose, 1991; Zborowski, 1952; Koopman, Eisenthal and Stoeckle, 1984; Lipton and Marbach, 1984; Calvillo and Flaskerud, 1993).

II A quantitative method, applied to a representative sample of patients at discharge, asking questions about pain control, identifying ethnic group and looking at any other salient factors, such as sex, age, health status, treatment, ward etc.

III If differences in satisfaction were found, a quantitative method – an audit of patient records – to find out whether there were differences in the amount and type of pain control drugs given to different ethnic categories of patient.

IV Depending on the result of (iii), a qualitative method – either to find out why some groups of patients feel less satisfied (perhaps because they feel more afraid, or have no one to talk to), or to find out why nurses behave differently towards some groups of patients.

This is not the only way that differences in ethnic responses to pain or nurses' attitudes to pain can be explored, and those wishing to carry out research in the area should consult the references given above.

Those who need further convincing about the relevance of this subject might be interested to know that studies have shown that nurses' perceptions of pain are different to those of patients. In fact, regardless of culture, in studies nurses gave less medication for pain than was ordered and less medication than patients needed to alleviate their pain. The goal of nurses was found to be to reduce patients' pain, not to relieve it (Cohen, 1980; Jacox, 1979; Teske, Daut and Cleeland, 1983; Rankin and Snider, 1984; Dudley and Holm, 1984).

Davitz and Davitz (1981) studied nurses' attitudes towards pain and found that a patient's ethnicity was related to how much physical and psychological distress the nurse believed the patient was experiencing. Nurses thought that Jewish and Spanish-speaking patients expressed the most distress with pain and Anglo-Saxon patients the least. Nurses' attitudes and responses to pain are extremely important, because if they feel that black patients are experiencing less pain than white patients but making more fuss about it, they may give them too little analgesic.

An example of a study which showed quite clearly that nurses evaluated pain differently for different ethnic groups is that carried out by Calvillo and Flaskerud (1993). They used the McGill Pain Questionnaire together with amount of analgesics and three physiological measures to measure pain in 60 patients, either Mexican American or Anglo American, following elective cholecystectomy. The nurse's assessment of patient pain was measured using the Present Pain Intensity Scale.

The researchers found no significant differences between Mexican American and Anglo American women's responses to cholecystectomy pain on any of the measures of pain. However, there was a significant difference between the two ethnic groups in pain scores as evaluated by the nurse, with Anglo American patients assessed as experiencing more pain. The researchers comment:

*A major finding of this study is that nurses are assigning more
pain to Anglo and to 'higher' social-class patients: those who were
more educated, had professional or skilled occupations, spoke
English, and were born in the US. It might be assumed that
patients with these social-class characteristics would also receive
more pain management, more attention, and more pain relief than
other patients. This finding might be interpreted cautiously that
nurses assign a greater amount of pain and more credibility to the
expression of pain in those patients with more social value.*

(Calvillo and Flaskerud, 1993)

Calvillo and Flaskerud also found that nurses evaluated pain as
less for all patients than patients did themselves, confirming
results found in other studies mentioned above.

Informal Methods

In addition to the traditional social science methods available,
a number of informal methods, such as patient representatives
and advocates, telephone helplines, patients councils,
consultation meetings, patient participation groups etc have
been developed in the health and social care setting, and these
can be a very valuable way of collecting information when used
in combination with the more formal methods.

Qualitative and informal methods do not demand a
representative sample of users or large numbers of respondents
because the aim is to explore in detail the range, variety and
depth of views, feelings and explanations. Care should be taken,
however, to include a typical spread of different types of people.

A range of methods are available within the main categories
outlined above, but not all of these are suitable for use with
black people. This is illustrated in the following section, which
gives examples of methods in use.

Effectiveness of Methods in Use

Structured Questionnaire and Interview Surveys

The evidence for what does not work is very clear. Surveys of the general population using postal self-completion questionnaires usually fail to collect the views of black people.

For example, researchers carrying out a postal survey of residents in the area served by Wycombe Health Authority achieved a 73 per cent response rate but they commented:

> *There was a total lack of interest on the part of ethnic minorities, despite requesting help from the local community liaison officer.*

> (Barr and Rogers, 1991)

There are least three possible reasons for the low response in circumstances such as the above example.

★   Black people form a very small proportion of the general population in many areas of the country.

★   They may lack the motivation to complete questionnaires, seeing no benefit to themselves.

★   Many may be unable to read the questionnaire because English is not their first language.

Where black people form a large proportion of the general population, the response to surveys is likely to be much lower than that found by Barr and Rogers. Bowling et al (1992) mailed 400 people with self-completion questionnaires and after three reminders received just 45 replies. However, they had anticipated this low response and were able to interview 265 of the non-respondents.

A way to overcome the first problem of low numbers in the local population is to target black communities, by selecting names and addresses in particular areas or getting local community liaison workers to hand them out at events attended by black people. These routes will not provide a random sample, but they are a way of attempting to get a larger response from people in these communities.

However, the response rate to postal self-completion questionnaires may still be low, even when different communities are targeted in this way.

For example, as part of a study aimed at improving accessibility and service delivery to black people in the Manor Gardens Centre catchment area of London, Ogunsola (1991) conducted a survey using a postal self-completion questionnaire. One hundred English language questionnaires were distributed but only 12 were returned, even though she used language helpers to distribute the questionnaires.

Half were given to language helpers at a 'Healthy Islington 2000 Weekend' at the Chequers Centre. The language helpers were asked to give them out and help people to complete them. The other half were distributed to black people at the Manor Gardens Centre and to women at an English language class where the teacher agreed to help the women complete the questionnaire.

The low response rate may have been due to the language helpers being too busy to concentrate on the task, or inexperienced at interviewing; or the venue or surroundings may have been unsuitable for questionnaire completion.

A higher response rate can be achieved if attenders at existing community group meetings are targeted, so that the venue is comfortable to the respondents and they are amongst friends. It also helps if the interpreters are well prepared and participants are given a clear explanation of why they are being asked to fill in a questionnaire.

For example, when Bowling et al (1992) explored the validity of involving members of local community groups in priority setting exercises as a method of consulting the public, they received completed questionnaires from 116 white European and 217 black people who answered an ethnic identity question out of the 350 completed questionnaires they received.

The questionnaires, which asked a range of questions including ones about treatment/service priorities, were given out at a routine meeting of each of the 27 community groups in City and Hackney which were attended in the main study. The number of attenders at each session who completed the questionnaire ranged from 6 to 51. Community group leaders assisted with the translation of the questionnaire into Turkish and Chinese languages, and with interpretation with Vietnamese and Asian languages.

Handing out self-completion questionnaires at meetings of community groups and using interpreters where necessary can produce a higher response rate, but this will not be a random or representative sample of the population because not everyone is a member of a community group. Bowling et al also interviewed a random sample of the population using the same questionnaire.

Translating postal self-completion questionnaires may produce a slightly higher response rate, as will targeting people who have recently used a service and so have health high on their agenda, but the increase is still not likely to be high enough to be reliable.

For example, Ahmad (1990) carried out an inpatient satisfaction survey, one of the aims of which was to compare the views of white and Asian patients about their stay in hospital. Approximately equal numbers of white and Asian patients were needed. In order to achieve his target of 125 patients in each group, a combination of approaches was used: postal questionnaires (accompanied by a translated letter to Asian patients) sent out within a week of discharge, and home interviews.

Of the 223 Asian patients selected for the postal survey, 64 usable questionnaires were returned after one (translated) reminder (a 29 per cent response rate). Of the 264 white patients selected for the postal survey, 131 usable questionnaires were returned after one reminder (a 50 per cent response rate).

In sum, it is best to avoid the postal self-completion questionnaire as a means of collecting quantitative information from black people.

The best method to use is the structured interview. This has been used very successfully in many studies (eg Rashid and Jagger, 1992; Hawthorne, 1990; Swarup, 1993; SMSR, 1992), although a number of aspects – such as (i) access to potential respondents, (ii) the use of interpreters, and (iii) the most relevant questions to ask – need to be planned carefully in advance.

Access to Potential Respondents

An appropriate sampling frame coupled with a high response rate (at least 70 per cent) is necessary to make the results of a quantitative survey reliable.

The sampling frame should contain the total population from which a sample will be taken. If a survey aims to get information from a representative sample of all the black people resident in a particular location (rather than a sample of all the population resident in that location) this will entail compiling a list of households of different ethnic origins.

From 1993 it has been easier to locate households using data from the 1991 Census, although certain groups may be under-represented owing to their having avoided filling in a census form.

It is possible to make a decent attempt at a local black sampling frame without using census data (or in combination with census data if necessary). For example, Swarup (1993) achieved one in South East Hampshire by the following means:

★ Local black community organisations were located and a good relationship established with them.

★ Membership lists comprising address and ethnic origin of household were made available to the researcher by those who kept them.

★ Other sources were approached to find households not involved in the community organisations. Most were unable to provide information because no ethnic monitoring was being carried out. The most fruitful sources were the Multicultural Education and Language Support Centre, local authority housing departments, health visitors, adult education language classes, black women's groups and the Community Liaison Unit.

★ Use was also made of the Electoral Register as a source of information. Volunteers from the different communities who were familiar with the names were recruited to help identify households from their particular community. This proved a 'long, tedious but eventually successful' task.

★ The various lists from the different sources were cross-referenced to produce one list for each ethnic group. Some households remained difficult to identify. This was particularly the case with groups originating from the Middle Eastern Countries (the Gulf war was imminent).

★ A 25 per cent structured random sample was taken from the total households identified in each black group.

The sampling frame appropriate for a particular survey will depend upon the aim of the research. If, for example, the views of inpatients on quality of hospital care are being sought, the sampling frame will be the total number of inpatients discharged over a particular period. This was the case for Ahmad (1990) in Rochdale.

The hospital concerned discharged approximately 70 or 80 patients daily, approximately 10 of these being of Asian origin, and roughly equal numbers of Asian and white patients were required for comparison purposes.

Every Asian name on the discharge list for each day was included but only every ninth white patient, until the required sample size of 250 was achieved.

However Ahmad found that the number of white patients chosen for the survey came to exceed the number of Asians, because the number of Asian patients admitted to the hospital during the month of the survey fell (it was April, linked to Ramadam and Eid).

Other possible sampling frames, depending on the aim of the survey, are the Electoral Register and FHSA lists of patients registered with GPs, but it is difficult to identify members of some ethnic groups by name from these lists (eg Black-Caribbean).

Identifying a suitable sampling frame, choosing an appropriate sample size (this will depend upon whether the results from different groups of people are to be compared, and the length of the questionnaire or interview schedule) are not the only important elements: motivating as many people in the sample as possible to respond is vital.

It is more motivating to be approached personally by an interviewer than it is to receive a self-completion questionnaire. However, it is unwise to assume that unprepared people will leap at the chance to be interviewed by someone knocking on their door. This is particularly the case if they are black and the interviewer is white. A white person is associated with 'the authority'.

There are two main ways of preparing people for an interview:

★ Increasing the chance that they will have heard about the research before they are contacted. This can be done through discussing the project with local community organisations, religious leaders etc, and by publicising the research in appropriate newspapers, shop windows etc.

★ Sending each household/person in the sample a (translated) letter giving details about the project and asking their permission to carry out an interview.

For example, researchers undertaking a study of uptake of health services by the Asian community in North West Surrey (Dumelow and Bailey, 1993) went through a number of stages before beginning their household interview survey.

★ Attending meetings of the Woking Community Relations Forum.

★ Discussions with 12 Asian Community Group organisers.

★ A meeting in the mosque with the Imam (who agreed to inform local people during prayers and encourage them to be involved in the study).

★ During 'One World Week' in 1991 the researcher took part in various multicultural events and designed and distributed over 200 leaflets in Woking town centre.

★ One week before visiting, a letter translated into three Asian languages was sent to each household in the sample of 330 detailing an approximate time and day of visit.

Using interviewers of the appropriate ethnic category is best, although the refusal rate in some groups may still be relatively high even when this procedure is adopted. Swarup (1993) found in her study that people in the Chinese community were more likely to refuse an interview than others. A Chinese community worker suggested that this was because many Chinese people did not like to be seen criticising any authority.

However, an interviewer who is able to set the respondent at ease on the doorstep by speaking the appropriate language and being culturally recognisable is an asset. Word is likely to get around that an interviewer who is 'OK' is conducting a survey, and suspicions will be allayed for those in the majority of groups.

A clear warning against using only white interviewers is given by Ahmad (1990). He found that:

> *... Once the contact was made and the purpose of the visit explained, no Asian or white patient refused to be interviewed by me ... However, when a white male interviewer tried to conduct some of the interviews in place of me he was unable to persuade the remaining Asian patients to be interviewed.*

(Ahmad, 1990, p. 61)

Using Interpreters

It is a difficult and time-consuming process to translate a structured questionnaire or interview schedule into a different language, and it may be a waste of time anyway because competent interviewers may speak a language but not read it. Also some interviewees may prefer a mixture of English and their first language.

If bilingual interviewers or interpreters are used, translation is not necessary because the interviewer can translate the question as they read it.

Interpreters or the bilingual people available may not be trained interviewers, however, and so they will need to be trained before becoming involved in the survey.

In the research carried out by SMSR (1992) in Dewsbury, the majority of the bilingual interviewers recruited were not experienced interviewers. The 15 interviewers were recruited from the districts where field work was to take place by personal contact. The qualifications required were:

> *... A personality suited to one to one interviewing, sensitivity in discussing personal issues, a respect for confidentiality and the ability to speak at least two Asian languages in addition to English.*
>
> (SMSR, 1992, p. 10)

The SMSR researchers identified the following elements of training and supervision as necessary:

★ Initial briefing on overall project aims and methods

★ Training in interviewing techniques, including role playing

★ Interviewing in Asian languages – translation issues

★ Briefing and debriefing prior to qualitative interviews (which took place before the interviews using the structured questionnaires)

★ Briefing and debriefing during the quantitative interviews (a number of sessions)

★ Consultation during strategy development

For reasons of security and ease of writing down responses, most interviewers in the SMSR survey worked in single sex pairs. A similar procedure took place in the Dumelow and Bailey (1993) study in North West Surrey, where one interpreter and one researcher visited each house to carry out the interviews. Here the interpreter carried out all the interviews (apart from those in English) and the interviewer recorded all responses and provided guidance where necessary.

A small scale check on the reliability of this way of translating questionnaires or interview schedules was conducted by SMSR. Eleven respondents were re-interviewed two days after the first interview and by a second interviewer.

Analysis of comparisons between the two completed questionnaires showed that most discrepancies existed in the case of questions where interviewers had already reported problems, principally through there being a lack of understanding of the concept which it was hoped to examine. The researchers remark:

> *A few questions created difficulties as they touched upon concepts that many respondents did not understand, either through lack of a parallel translation or ignorance of the workings of the Health Service. Explanation by the interviewers generally managed to make the concept clear and most of the questions were so fundamental to the study that it would have been wrong to omit them.*

(SMSR, 1992, p. 18)

Swarup (1991) also reported that certain words were difficult to translate into some languages. She commented that interviewers with the same language were able to help each other out and find ways of interpreting such terms.

Relevancy of Questions

It is clear that the different language and cultural backgrounds of many minority ethnic groups make certain concepts familiar to health professionals difficult to understand.

This problem is not confined to minority groups, and many researchers have shown that lay concepts of health and lay understanding of certain medical terms can be completely different from those of health professionals (eg Calnan, 1988; Blumhagen, 1980; Hadlow and Pitts, 1991).

Difficulties in the understanding of certain questions should be picked up during the piloting of questionnaires and interview schedules. A pilot (of 10–20 people) is essential for two reasons.

First, it will be possible to find out whether the questions are understandable and mean the same to the respondent as they do to the interviewer. Any changes can then be made before the main survey.

Secondly, by looking at the responses it will be possible to see whether the questions are going to provide useful information – that is, whether they are worth asking. If everyone appears to be responding 'highly satisfied' to a question, or 'don't know', it may be better to omit this question or tackle that particular issue in another way.

Piloting the questionnaires can highlight other potential problems too. For example, the SMSR researchers found that the interviews took much longer than they had anticipated. This was because of the amount of highly specific translation or interpretation and explanation of concepts required. The researchers add:

> *In view of these problems, accentuated by the willingness of respondents to speak at length once their confidence had been gained, it was decided to pay interviewers at a higher rate than had been planned.*

(SMSR, 1992, p. 15)

How are questions constructed in the first instance? This will depend upon the aim of the research, but in many cases, and particularly where health needs or users' views of the service are concerned, it is essential to use a qualitative method such as unstructured interviews or discussion groups first, in order to find out what these issues look like from the users' point of view.

Lay people and service users usually have a very different perception than professional people of what constitutes a good quality service and what are health priorities. Questions that reflect only the health professionals' view point are likely to collect inappropriate information (see McIver, 1993a, for further information).

Unstructured Interviews

The aim of all qualitative research, including unstructured interviews, is to find out what aspects of life are like from the respondents' point of view.

This type of interviewing demands more skill from the interviewer than the structured method because they must frame their own questions spontaneously in response to the information provided. Neither the questions asked nor the interviewer's body language must lead the respondent, yet the interviewer must be able to guide the respondent to talk about issues relevant to the study.

Large numbers of people are not required, any number between 15 and 75 being typical. A representative sample of people is not needed either, although a good mix of different categories of people is required. The exact mix will depend upon the research aim.

If the aim is to discover perceptions of Afro-Caribbean women about health and health services, as was Thorogood's (1989, 1992) for example, age may have an important influence on views; and in this case the researcher drew her sample of 32 women from two age groups: 16–30 years and 40–60 years.

The source of the sample should also be varied so that a range of views is collected. Thorogood drew hers from the GP waiting room of a local health centre and by word of mouth recommendations from the community.

A varied sample of people is ideal, but as qualitative methods are often used for exploratory research, getting access to a selection of appropriate people can sometimes be very difficult and the researcher may be pleased to be able to interview anyone at all.

For example, in 1987 the Birmingham Community Care Special Action Project ran a series of consultation meetings with carers for the city council in order to develop a carer's programme.

These meetings were unsuccessful in attracting significant participation by more than a handful of either Afro-Caribbean or Asian carers, despite the availability of interpreters, and contact with community groups, temples, mosques etc

As a consequence a project was set up by the Community Care Special Action Project and the King's Fund Centre to increase understanding about the needs of carers from black communities.

A wide variety of approaches was tried in order to identify carers, including:

★   Visits to local voluntary and statutory agencies with requests to workers to distribute a letter to carers asking for their help with the project. This produced a minimal response.

★   Distribution of a leaflet to churches, community centres, home-based groups, temples, mosques and advice centres. There was no direct response from carers to the leaflet but it did raise enquiries from community workers about the initiative.

★   Advertising in the form of a jingle, which was played on every programme, 24 hours a day for two weeks, by a local radio station targeting the black community in Birmingham. This produced no direct response.

★   Attempts via churches, temples and mosques to contact carers. These also proved unsuccessful.

Contacts established via service providers were more successful. A carers' assessment unit for children with learning difficulties and a day care centre for people with physical disabilities were visited. Staff from the units agreed to help by providing names and addresses of carers. Letters were sent to the carers explaining the purpose of the research and appointments were arranged.

Joint visits with community nurses from the local team working with people with learning difficulties were also arranged. Linkworkers attached to minority ethnic health projects proved another effective means of contacting Asian carers. The researchers comment:

> *In this and other projects the evidence is that leaflets, posters and local media do not in themselves encourage carers to come forward to be interviewed or to take part in a 'research project'. What does seem to be important is the patient and careful building up of relationships with a variety of individuals in different networks who then act as intermediaries.*

(Jowell, Larrier and Lawrence, 1990)

Researchers can also use a method known as 'snowballing' to contact individuals who may not be in contact with statutory or voluntary services. This entails asking a respondent already identified to introduce them to others they know who are in a similar position to themselves.

This can be a slow process and relies heavily on the ability of the interviewer to convince the respondent that the research is valuable and confidential. It works better in situations where people are part of informal networks (eg users of illegal drugs) than where people are isolated.

Discussion Groups

There are many different kinds of 'discussion groups' but their use as a research method is quite distinct. Usually termed 'focus groups' or 'focused group discussions', guidance on their use in a health service setting can be found in the Shropshire HA/ University of Birmingham publication (1992) *Getting to the Core* (see also, generally, Goldmann and McDonald, 1987; Krueger, 1988; Walker, 1985).

The advantage of using such groups is that many people find it difficult to express themselves spontaneously in the interview situation but may be 'drawn out' amongst people who have gone through similar experiences. Also, as part of a group they may find that their experiences are given shape and form in the words of others and so be better able to express their own views.

Discussion groups do not work for issues where social pressure may influence views or where the subject may be embarrassing to participants. Also, subjects cannot be covered in as much individual detail as in the interview.

The recruitment of participants can be difficult, because people are being asked to leave their homes and give as much as two or three hours of their time to take part in a project. Clearly they must be convinced of the value of the project and of their contribution before they will participate. The convenience and familiarity of the setting can also be important in encouraging participation.

An important feature of focus groups is that the participants in a group should be matched for similarity across certain variables if these are likely to influence their opinions. This is so that different types of opinion can be distinguished and not lost as they might be if they were all present in one group. Ethnic group is obviously one such variable, so it would be necessary to hold separate discussion groups with members of different ethnic groups if the needs or views of different groups were being explored. Sex, age and socio-economic status may also be important variables.

A good example of the use of discussion groups to collect qualitative information from black people is provided by the work of Shah, Harvey and Coyle (1993). As part of a project initiated and partly funded by South Glamorgan HA, to determine the health and social care needs of minority ethnic people in South Glamorgan, a series of 14 focused group discussions took place.

This was double the number of groups initially envisaged, as:

★ It was difficult to make a decision about which groups to target and which to omit. It was decided therefore to target only the largest minority groups. However, within the 'Asian' category there were four large groups (Bengali, Gujerati, Pakistani, Punjabi) and as it was impossible to choose between these, all four were targeted.

★ For each group chosen, sex was felt to be an important differentiating category, so focus groups were conducted separately for men and women (except in one of the Chinese and Afro-Caribbean groups, where men turned up so a mixed discussion was held).

The discussions took place in locations which were comfortable to the participants – places of worship, community centres, health centres, the Community Education Centre, the Barnado's Multicultural Resource Centre and a Chinese restaurant.

The researchers remark that 'recruitment of participants was extremely difficult'. Eventually, after a pilot session, it was decided to give each participant £5 for expenses incurred in attending. All participants were assured of total confidentiality.

All contact with participants was made through 'key informers' and via introductions. Usually it is recommended that group participants should be unknown to each other so there is no shared knowledge hidden from the facilitators. This was difficult to achieve under the circumstances, but some prior acquaintance proved to be an advantage, in that discussions were found to flow better.

Interpreters were used in the sessions where the language of the group was not familiar to the research officer. During the sessions the interpreter usually provided an update on progress every 5–10 minutes. All sessions were taped and where necessary a translated transcript was provided by the interpreter afterwards.

In the opinion of the researchers this process of using an interpreter to relay questions and summarise answers was successful but did have drawbacks.

A problem that can occur is that the interpreters may not always translate every comment made, so some comments can be missed. The researchers felt, however, that it was important wherever possible to use professionally trained interviewers who spoke the appropriate language. They also comment:

> With hindsight, the only difference we would make in undertaking a similar survey, is allocating additional time spans for the completion of such work.

(Shah, Harvey and Coyle, 1993, p. 100)

Observation

Sometimes actions and behaviour are below the conscious level of awareness and so may not be described clearly in interviews. In these instances it is useful to watch and record what happens.

An example is the research on midwives' attitudes to South Asian descent maternity patients carried out by Bowler (1993). The main research method here was observation, although this was supported by interviews with 25 midwives.

A good illustration of the way in which observation can help to provide an insight into 'taken for granted' behaviour which may be causing problems is given during her examination of communication difficulties.

The level of competence in English among the Asian women observed was generally low and this resulted in the women being characterised as unresponsive, rude and unintelligent by the midwives.

During the observation it became clear that the midwives were making the situation worse because they were using euphemisms which confused the Asian women even further.

In one instance, when the researcher had accompanied a community midwife on a home visit, the midwife needed to examine the woman to see whether her uterus had begun to contract back to its previous size. This meant that the woman had to be asked if she needed to empty her bladder.

> *Midwife:　Do you need to go to the toilet – pass water?*
> *Rubina:　Yes.*
> *Midwife:　Or have you just been?*
> *Rubina:　Yes.*
>
> *Rubina looked confused and went out of the room, only to return immediately with an empty specimen bottle and an interrogative look on her face. The midwife waved it away crossly, told Rubina to lie on the sofa and began to feel her stomach.*
>
> (Bowler, 1993, p. 162)

The phrases 'pass water' and 'have you just been?' did not make the question about needing to 'go to the toilet' any easier for the woman to understand.

The midwife seemed to have no idea she was making the situation more difficult for herself and her patient, yet guidelines do exist on speaking clearly and simply to aid communication with those whose first language is not English (eg Henley, 1988). This subject will be returned to in Chapter 5, 'Developing Culturally Sensitive Services'.

Informal Methods

Consultation

Meetings of many different kinds have been used with varying success within the NHS to obtain information from service users. 'Consultation' is a word used to describe many of these attempts.

There are two main ways of carrying out consultation meetings: (i) using meetings of particular community groups to discuss issues; and (ii) arranging special meetings to which members of different community groups are invited.

(i) Community Group Meetings

An example is provided by Ogunsola (1991) who carried out nine consultations with community groups, as part of her research aimed at improving accessibility and service delivery to black people in the Manor Gardens Centre catchment area in London.

The groups concerned covered a variety of communities, including African, Afro-Caribbean, Asian, Greek-Cypriot and Turkish. Many were small and catered to particular sections of a community (eg the Tollington Way Afro Caribbean Pensioners Lunch Club).

The procedure adopted to consult with community groups where English was understood and spoken was to ask questions and write the group's response on a flipchart so that members of the group could add to and query the notes as they were being taken. Groups were asked to:

★   Describe themselves.

★   List the services at the Manor Gardens Centre that they had used (this involved a review of the services available).

★ List the good things about the services they had used.

★ List the things that were not so good about the services they had used.

★ Say which services they had not used but did want to use, and why they had not used them yet.

★ Say what they felt needed to be done in order to:
  – improve services for them;
  – make services easier for them to use;
  – make services appropriate to people in the group.

★ Say how they felt about ethnic monitoring.

★ Say what cultural practices they would like the Manor Gardens Centre clinic staff to be aware of.

In five of the consultations the majority of people in the group did not speak English. Where workers in the groups acted as interpreters the sessions were longer and not as comprehensive as those in which the group understood English.

In one group a worker took responsibility for conducting the session and only referred to the researcher for more information about services available. In this case the flipchart notes made by the worker were not as comprehensive as those made in the other consultation sessions, although the discussion had been quite lively and lengthy.

The experience of Ogunsola shows that details about the health needs and experiences of different ethnic groups, and those of different ages, sex and circumstances within these groups, are more likely to be discovered by contacting the smaller community organisations, rather than relying solely on the larger, more well established voluntary organisations.

It may take some time to discover these small organisations but a directory, once compiled, will be useful to those in a number of voluntary and statutory agencies.

The experience of Ogunsola also shows that when arranging meetings with groups that are likely to comprise non-English speakers it is advisable to take along a trained bilingual interpreter/interviewer to make sure that the session proceeds smoothly and the information collected is as comprehensive as possible.

(ii) Specially Arranged/Public Meetings

An example is provided by Parkside Health Authority, who carried out an initial round of consultation meetings in August/September 1991 as part of ongoing work to establish a consultation process to help improve service delivery to black groups in the district (Silvera, 1992).

The meetings were borough based and were structured around four care groups (physical disability services, maternity services, HIV/AIDS services, and services for the elderly). Four meetings were held in each borough. The meetings were timed so that the issues that arose could be incorporated into the consultation on the purchasing authority's purchasing plan for 1992–93.

Publicity information was sent to over 400 groups, agencies and individuals. These included local community groups, voluntary agencies, health workers, individuals with a specific interest in the health of black people, FHSAs, local authorities, the Community Health Council and other local agencies.

Venues familiar to community groups and voluntary agencies were chosen in each borough to host the consultation meetings. Each venue accommodated four meetings focusing on one of the priority care group areas.

The interest expressed in the consultation in terms of numbers of people attending the meetings was very low in comparison with the amount of information sent out. An assumption was made that 20–30 people would attend each meeting, but in the event the highest attendance was 25 and the lowest 4.

Silvera (1992) puts forward a list of explanations for the low attendance, some of which were comments made by agencies contacted by telephone prior to the meetings:

★ Agencies were not given sufficient time.

★ Publicity information was not clear.

★ The agenda offered was too rigid.

★ Agencies were not familiar with the health authority conducting such events.

★ Black issues were not a priority for many voluntary groups and community agencies.

★ Too many meetings were organised.

★ Insufficient 'ground work' had been done in the community to promise interest in a public consultation exercise.

★ Publicity information only targeted groups and agencies and not users.

★ Not all the possible forms of publicity had been used (eg local community radio and the local press).

★ Many groups and agencies did not work in the specific areas of interest publicised.

★ Health issues are not a priority for many groups and agencies.

★ Some had had bad past experience of attempts at consultation by statutory bodies.

★ The timing of the consultation exercise was bad (many people were away on holiday).

★ Community agencies had insufficient staff.

Clearly public consultation meetings need to be organised very carefully if they are to draw good attendance. A combination of attending meetings of existing groups and arranging special meetings would seem to be a good idea.

Both Ogunsola (1991) and Silvera (1992), along with other writers, offer advice on good practice in consultation. Much of this advice is also relevant to the use of other methods for obtaining information from black people and has been mentioned in earlier sections of this book. Some key issues are:

★   Links with local communities should be established before consultation takes place.

★   A clear message regarding the reason for consulting local communities should be given. This should contain a commitment to take action on feedback from the consultation process, and this commitment should be demonstrated early on because of the history of past inaction after similar activities.

★   Consultation should be ongoing, rather than a 'one-off' exercise, and should take place in different ways and different settings to give different people and communities the opportunity to take part. The procedures for consultation need to be clear and accessible to different black communities.

★   Specific communities should be targeted, and there should not be too much reliance on umbrella groups. Opportunities should be made for groups to make representation to the health authority directly.

★   The infra-structure of the black voluntary sector needs to be developed if it is to fulfil its potential. This development should include funding for training, management education and consultancies.

    Those within it need help in identifying and formulating their position on various issues and in acting as a link or communication channel between the health authority or hospital and the community.

Reports of visits to hospitals by black members who can act as interpreters and so communicate with a wide range of people could be an additional source of information about service quality. For example, Camberwell CHC carried out a visit 'to determine whether the cultural, dietary, religious and communication needs of patients at Dulwich Hospital are being met' (Camberwell CHC, 1992).

They were able to make several recommendations, including that 'the authenticity of Halal meat served in the hospital should be confirmed by stamping or certification of each food pack' – a small and inexpensive change which managers might consider trivial but which would be of great significance to those who only eat Halal food (see also the section 'Diet' in Chapter 5, 'Developing Culturally Sensitive Services').

Health Advocates, Linkworkers and Interpreters

An increasing number of staff are being employed by health organisations to improve communication between service purchasers/providers and patients/local black communities. Although supplying information to managers and other health professionals about patients' views is not generally within their remit, they are often a useful source of information on the service experiences and views of those they work with or advocate on behalf of.

However, there is some confusion over the various job titles and responsibilities of postholders. Some are being employed only to interpret, others are expected to interpret and also advocate on behalf of the client, and others to interpret and carry out development work or research.

Although advocacy is developing slowly in the UK, examples of different types of advocacy do exist, and some of these initiatives are concerned with black people. One such is the Hackney Multi-Ethnic Women's Health Project started in 1980.

Information about health authority/organisation structures and how health staff link with each other and across departments should be produced so that these groups know how to link with the statutory sector.

★ Issues for consultation should be developed jointly, rather than the community being informed of what they will be. This encourages ownership and participation on both sides.

★ The objectives of each consultation exercise should be clearly laid out and the effectiveness of the process analysed after the exercise so that limitations can be recognised and improvements can occur.

Many writers feel that the establishment of black groups is a good way to help members of these communities develop a 'voice' to engage in the dialogue initiated by the health sector.

Two main types of group have been suggested – (i) groups of service users or ex-users (user groups), and (ii) 'umbrella' community groups (health forums) – but these are not the only models.

An example of a different type of 'umbrella' organisation is the Manchester Action Committee on Health Care for Ethnic Minorities (MACHEM), which was set up to influence health services and local authorities to make services more appropriate and accessible for members of black communities (MACHEM, 1991; Changing Health Services, 1992).

MACHEM has grown from an informal grouping in 1987 to become an independent, broad based, multi-ethnic alliance, with a membership of 67 groups and individuals. It has two part-time development workers and an administrator.

Some independent organisations have had difficulty in establishing links with statutory agencies and so in creating opportunities to influence decision-making, but MACHEM has, over time, succeeded in establishing formal links with three

District Health Authorities, one FHSA, a number of NHS trusts, and a purchasing consortium set up by the District Health Authorities in Greater Manchester.

Evidence that these links are taken seriously by senior managers in the organisations concerned can be found in MACHEM's Annual Report 1990–91, which contains reports by the Chief Executives of the Manchester Central Hospitals and Community Care NHS Trust and North and South Manchester Health Authorities.

Commenting on MACHEM's progress, during a conference in 1992, Kais Uddin remarked:

> *In general, practical work has been patchy, but it has resulted in some improvements to services ... MACHEM has survived essentially because of the energy and commitment of a small core group of people – not in all cases the same group over the whole period ... Another important factor has been expertise; it has been crucial that membership included health authority workers and officers, who were able to tell us how the system worked, how to make it work, and what was happening inside it.*

> (Changing Health Services, 1992)

Community Health Councils

Since 1974 the statutory role of 'people's watchdog' in the NHS has been given to the Community Health Councils (CHCs). Gathering information about local views on NHS services through various mechanisms including surveys, complaints and visits, and reporting this information to the health organisations concerned, has been a major part of their workload.

However, there has been limited black representation on CHCs, so many are not in touch with the needs of these communities. Cautions about relying too heavily on CHCs at the expense of direct involvement from black communities have come from a number of directions.

For example, in an evaluation of the Asian Mother and Baby Campaign (Rocheron, Dickinson and Khan, 1989) the writer comment that in the three districts studied in detail:

> *Observations of the Steering Committee meetings suggest that the presence of the Community Health Council cannot compensate for the lack of Asian Community participation, nor should Community Health Council involvement be thought of as a substitute for Asian Community participation.*

> (Rocheron, Dickinson and Khan, 1989, p. 13)

Having said this, the picture has begun to change, and a numb of CHCs have set up Black and Minority Ethnic Working Partie and are trying to recruit members from different community groups.

Many CHCs are also in the process of reviewing their workload to bring it up to date with the recent NHS reforms. One approach which seems to be emerging as particularly useful is monitoring services through visits. CHCs have the right to visit premises managed by their local district health authority and those of NHS trusts within the district.

A booklet entitled *Effective Visiting for Community Health Councils* (Joule and Levenson, 1992) produced by the Greater London Association of CHCs gives four reasons why visiting is particularly relevant to the current situation. It is a way of:

★ Gathering information in order to monitor DHA contracts

★ Revealing gaps in service provision and uncovering problems of access to a service for particular groups

★ Raising awareness amongst patients and staff of issues such as the role of the CHC, service standards, and complaints procedure

★ Involving CHC members in the work of the organisation

This project was funded by the Inner City Partnership and is administered by the City and Hackney CHC, which means that it operates independently of the local health authority (Cornwell and Gordon, 1984).

A few projects have a more general health brief. Leeds City Council, for example, employs a patient advocate and ten volunteer patient advocates from different cultures, to support patients in hospitals and clinics throughout Leeds and the surrounding area. The scheme was started in 1987 in order to help patients put forward their views and wishes to health staff, particularly in obstetrics, paediatrics and mental health (Holmes, 1991).

From the health service manager's point of view, independent advocacy schemes do not easily provide information which can be used to develop service quality. An advocate's primary concern is to represent the wishes of each individual patient to the health care provider concerned.

As they are independent they are likely to be outside the quality management system. This means that in order to make use of information from health advocates, managers have to find a way of encouraging advocates to collect and collate details of the problems they encounter during their work and then feed this information into the organisation's quality review process at regular intervals.

Linkworkers can be clearly distinguished from advocates, because they are employed by a health service or hospital to act as a 'go-between' or link between patients and staff. They are not employed solely to advocate on behalf of patients, but to help both patients and staff.

In the Asian Mother and Baby Campaign, linkworkers 'acted as a link between Asian women and health care professionals' and were trained 'to act as interpreters, cultural ambassadors, representatives of patients and staff, and health educators' (Rocheron, Dickinson and Khan, 1989).

The evaluators discovered that linkworkers found it difficult to represent the wishes of both health professionals and clients, and in practice the role of the linkworker was defined first by the health professional to whom she was accountable, and second by her client.

This is an issue which needs to be worked through, but it does not necessarily place the linkworker in an untenable position. The role of the patient representative or patient liaison officer, acting as a link between patients and staff with the aim of making services more sensitive to patients' needs, is one which has worked successfully for over 20 years in the USA and is currently being developed in a number of hospitals in the UK.

The concept of the patient representative originated in the USA in the late 1960s, and many early appointments had the aim of improving access for particular sections of the community. For example, describing the establishment of the first programme at the Mount Sinai Hospital, New York City, Ruth Ravich writes:

> *Its aim was to improve access to hospital services for our patients who came from all over the city, and most particularly for the East Harlem Community, our neighbours, most of whom were disadvantaged economically and encountered difficulties overcoming the institutional barriers appropriate to medical care.*

(Ravich, 1981)

A project funded by the Department of Health and managed by the National Association of Health Authorities and Trusts was set up in 1992 to develop the concept of the patient representative within the UK context. There are two pilot sites, at Frenchay Healthcare Trust and Brighton Healthcare, and information is being collected on similar posts elsewhere (McIver, 1993c).

Evidence from patient representative schemes in the USA shows that they are useful in helping provide personalised care, sorting out patients' problems before they become serious complaints, and helping in risk management and quality improvement programmes (see eg Sax, 1979; Lieber, 1977).

Both linkworkers and patient representatives are in a good position to provide information about how services can be improved from the patients' point of view but this cannot happen unless a formal procedure exists, such as quarterly reports to the Chief Executive or Board.

Unfortunately sometimes the responsibilities of interpreters, advocates or linkworkers are not clear. To employ an interpreter who is really expected to be an advocate, or to call a linkworker or patient representative a 'patient advocate' is a mistake because it may confuse three distinct tasks, all of which are important:

I   Access to an interpreter is a basic necessity for non-English speaking patients, without which several of the rights and standards in the Patient's Charter cannot be fulfilled.

II   An advocate is useful for patients who are in a disadvantaged position and so have difficulty making their views known (eg people with learning difficulties, mentally distressed people, black people), or are experiencing a problem with a health service and having difficulty getting a satisfactory resolution.

III A patient representative or linkworker can help to personalise services, create links with the local community, improve access, deal with the day to day problems of patients before they become complaints, and feed information about patients' problems directly into a quality improvement system.

All three roles can operate together, with workers referring patients to their colleagues where necessary.

Another factor contributing to the success of these posts is whether other staff know about the responsibilities of the new worker and how they relate to their own, so that they do not feel threatened.

The evaluators of the Asian Mother and Baby Campaign found that some staff 'denied the need for linkworkers because they had always managed to deliver care without them in the past' (Rocheron, Dickinson and Khan, 1989).

Patient representatives have also found that staff were initially hostile to them, fearing that they were a 'spy in the camp' or were taking over aspects of their work. Many health professionals consider themselves to be 'the patient's advocate', and so cannot understand why staff with special responsibilities in the area have been appointed.

Where black patients are concerned this resentment is likely to be increased by feelings that these patients should not receive 'special treatment' but should be 'treated the same' in order to avoid racism (the 'colour blind' approach).

One way to lessen this conflict is to provide staff with good reasons for the appointment and let them know how they can liaise with the new worker. Linkworkers and patient representatives have reported that it takes time to build relationships with other staff and to get established (six months to one year), but that once this has been achieved they are able to work more effectively.

With this knowledge it makes sense to employ workers on contracts no shorter than two years and longer if possible. It also helps if they have the opportunity to network with others in similar roles so that they can learn from others and build upon shared experience. Various support networks exist (see 'Useful Addresses').

Other Informal Methods

There are many other ways of using informal mechanisms to collect information about the needs and views of black people. Too little use is made of complaints, helplines, the observations of front line staff and development workers, and opportunities to collect information as well as give it, such as health education sessions.

Many managers and health professionals feel that these routes are useless because the information is unrepresentative. However, if it is recorded and collated regularly, analysed to detect patterns and used together with information gathered in other ways, it can back up and supplement information collected using traditional research methods.

Summary

This chapter has examined a wide variety of ways of collecting the views, opinions and needs of black people. Choice of method will depend upon factors such as the questions which need answering (whether they ask 'how many?' or 'why?'), knowledge of and access to the particular minority ethnic groups concerned, and the budget, resources and skills available.

Many managers are tempted to buy in consultancies to carry out sophisticated quantitative surveys, but before such decisions are made it is worth asking whether this is really necessary. Surveys are expensive and may not be the most effective way to improve services because they are time-consuming to carry out and the statistics must be translated into an action plan before changes in services can be made.

Surveys do have their place (see Cartwright, 1988, for examples of how surveys can be used to good effect), when carried out by experienced people; but other, less 'high tech', solutions should also be considered.

A good example is provided by a community care development group at Birmingham Social Services Department who wanted to develop culturally sensitive services for Chinese people. This example is particularly interesting because many conducting surveys have found Chinese people to be reluctant to give their views (eg Swarup, 1993). It also concerns minority ethnic carers, a group more difficult than most to contact (Jowell, Larrier and Lawrence, 1990).

The workers concerned (McPherson, 1992) identified five different voluntary groups within the Chinese community. They were careful not to focus on any one particular subgroup but to seek the views of those from Hong Kong, the Chinese Mainland and Taiwan, from the different religious groups (Buddhists, Christians and Ancestor Worshippers) and language groups (Cantonese, Hakka and Mandarin), and from rural and urban backgrounds.

They found that Chinese elders and their carers wanted day care, respite care, home care services and long term residential care that is culturally sensitive and appropriate.

A day centre for Chinese elderly people was planned through regular meetings with representatives from the Chinese community. A Chinese social work student helped to set up the day centre, and a social worker supervised the student and worked with the manager responsible for the day centre.

The day centre was to have 20 places and be open one day a week. The workers were advised that Tuesday was a day on which restaurants were closed and was therefore the best day on which to offer care.

Publicity attracted over 100 people to the opening day, and the next Tuesday 50 Chinese elders turned up. Places were offered following a needs-based social work assessment with interviews conducted with the help of a Cantonese speaker from a voluntary organisation.

Transport is provided to the centre but they also operate a luncheon club and drop-in centre for anyone who can make their own way.

Chinese videos are shown and elderly people play Mah-Jong. There are posters of Chinese festivals on the walls. Chinese crockery is used, round tables have replaced the square ones, and traditional food is served. Some members of staff are Chinese and speak Cantonese, and Chinese volunteers and relatives attend with their families and friends.

Day care has led to a take-up of other services by the elders, including respite care. The workers comment:

> *When we began this project we had no idea of the size of need within the Chinese community. But we did know that there was not a single Chinese person in any of the City's Social Services department's day centres.*

(McPherson, 1992)

In many cases research is not necessary because enough is already known about how changes can be effected to improve services to cater to the needs of black people. Examples of areas where this is the case are given in Chapter 5, 'Developing Culturally Sensitive Services'.

4 ETHNIC MONITORING

Ethnic monitoring collects information about utilisation of services, rather than users' opinions about services, but it is directly related to research on users' views because similar methodological issues must be tackled if it is to be successful.

One issue concerns the fact that ethnic monitoring records information collected from users on a questionnaire or form, so success is dependent upon the effective distribution and completion of these forms.

Health service staff are more likely to hand out questionnaires if they are convinced they are doing so for a useful purpose. They will be more reluctant if they feel it is ethically wrong, or 'just bureaucracy', or if they are embarrassed or lack confidence in the procedure for some reason.

Support for ethnic monitoring should not be taken for granted. Powerful arguments have been put forward both for and against inclusion of an 'ethnic question' in routine data collection, particularly for the 1981 and 1991 Censuses (Leech, 1989; Ahmad, 1990). Staff involved may benefit from an opportunity to work through these arguments, both for and against, during training sessions.

Those asked questions about their ethnic origin or asked to fill in forms requesting details of it, may well be worried about what the information will be used for, and may refuse. This is especially likely to happen if the request is unexpected.

A second methodological issue concerns the fact that questionnaires and similar forms are only as useful as the questions they ask. The value of statistical data, such as that collected during ethnic monitoring, is in collation and comparison with similar data collected at previous times or in other locations. This means it its best to use 'standard' or comparable categories.

In 1991, the Census asked a question about ethnic group for the first time. The classification of black groups adopted in the Census was extensively pre-tested by the Office of Population Census and Surveys (OPCS) through field studies. This provides the basis for a 'standard' set of categories:

★   White
★   Black – Caribbean
★   Black – African
★   Black – Other (please describe)
★   Indian
★   Pakistani
★   Bangladeshi
★   Chinese
★   Any other ethnic group (please describe)

These categories have met with some resistance in the 1991 Census and they may not be detailed enough for some parts of the country. It is possible to introduce further detail into the same framework to enable comparison. Andrew Kent of the Department of Health writes (1992):

> *If individual authorities or units wish to pursue further classification to reflect more accurately the ethnic mix of their community, the OPCS coding frame provides a further 26 classifications that can be used to analyse the* Other (please describe) *category.*

(Kent, 1992)

A third methodological issue is the way in which information collected is monitored and used to inform further research and decisions about changes to services.

Collection does not guarantee use, as was found by a survey of social service departments with an ethnic record keeping and monitoring system in 1990. Of the 40 departments that had such a system, only 14 had analysed their information (Butt, 1992).

To justify the collection of data on ethnic origin, the data should be used to improve services and access to services for black groups. This will entail linking data on utilisation of services by black groups to the findings of other research, such as research on patients' views.

Since April 1993 hospitals have been required by the Department of Health to collect data on the ethnicity of patients and day cases, and it is likely that this will spread to other service areas in the near future. There are practical difficulties in establishing ethnic monitoring, and guidance is being developed. Key collection procedures have been identified by the Department of Health. These are:

★ Self-categorisation by the patient
★ Ensuring the patient is asked for information only once
★ Handling questions and objections
★ Satisfying confidentiality concerns

Further information and guidance about ethnic monitoring can be found in Gunaratnam (1993) and Ogunsola (1992).

In sum, ethnic monitoring should be closely linked to research on users' views. Without data about ethnic origin, it is difficult to find out how many people from which ethnic groups are using health services, and whether ethnicity has relevance in other areas such as type of treatment, amount of pain relief and outcome.

This type of information is necessary if inequalities in access and treatment and care are to be reduced. As with all research and information collection, however, it is the use to which the information is put which is the real key to improvement, and ethnic monitoring will be merely a bureaucratic procedure unless the information is collated, examined, and used for research and as a basis for change.

5 DEVELOPING CULTURALLY SENSITIVE SERVICES

There is a surprisingly large amount of information already available which shows how services could be improved from the point of view of black people.

Plenty of research has already taken place and the same priority areas emerge every time, whatever the ethnic group or service concerned. These are: (i) communication, (ii) information provision, (iii) diet, and (iv) religious and cultural needs (see eg Swarup, 1993; Shah, Harvey and Coyle, 1993; Dumelow and Bailey, 1993; Slater, 1993; Larbie, 1985; GPMH, 1992; Bloomsbury HA, 1984).

These areas will be examined in more detail in this chapter, drawing upon examples from a range of service areas, such as maternity and mental health, and also looking at particular age groups, such as elderly people and children.

However, it is beyond the scope of the present publication to examine in detail the health needs and views on services of specific black communities. Some groups such as refugees, have slightly different health needs (on the subject of refugees and health: NW/NE Thames RHAs, 1992; Haringey HA, 1992;

Ruddy, 1992; and information provided by the Refugee Council – see 'Useful Addresses').

It is worth considering first what is meant by the phrase 'providing culturally sensitive care'.

The first point to make is that the NHS is not a culturally neutral organisation. As an organisation within a particular type of society, it reflects the culture (learned values, norms, beliefs and behaviours) of the cultural majority.

These cultural values tend to dominate in most areas, particularly in the popular media – television and daily newspapers – and so continue to be reinforced.

Sickness, childbirth and death are among the issues understood differently by those in different cultures, so health care providers cannot avoid paying attention to these areas if they are to provide acceptable care to all their patients.

Norms, beliefs, values and behaviours tend to be taken for granted and so lie below the conscious level of awareness. This means that unless trained to do otherwise, care givers tend to try to treat everyone in the same way, despite the fact that this will be inappropriate for some.

Inappropriate care can occur in a number of different ways. These may be fairly obvious, as in the use of white stitching material to sew up black skin, or prescription to Muslims of medicines derived from pigs.

Less obvious are the use of inappropriate assessment forms or tests, such as dementia scoring systems which are not relevant to ethnic elderly people (Darby, 1989); or provision of play and play equipment which does not reflect the experience of children from black families (Slater, 1993); or antenatal classes which do not discuss concepts of health and health care shared by black women (Larbie, 1985).

Just as the views of minority ethnic patients may be different to those of care providers on many issues, so also white patients may hold different views on some issues, particularly on what is meant by ill health and sickness.

This is because professional training and working in a particular environment can encourage a person to think and understand in a distinctive way. Research has shown that professional and lay views are different in many areas, such as health care priorities (Bowling, 1993; Dun, 1989) and what constitutes good primary health care (Smith and Armstrong, 1989) and health and illness (Molzahn and Northcott, 1989).

In recognising (a) that they are the product of a particular culture and have taken for granted assumptions that many patients may not share, and (b) that this means it is important to find out a patient's perceptions, expectations and understanding about issues such as illness and treatment, health care providers will be laying a foundation for culturally sensitive care for *all* patients.

The fact is, many issues are of concern to all patients, not just those from black communities, although additional aspects may apply for black patients.

For example, patients sometimes complain about staff ordering them around and making them feel like a number or an object, rather than a person. Black people may make the additional complaint that staff made racist comments, such as:

> *You black people have too many babies.*
>
> (Larbie, 1985, p. 19)

The issue here is a broad one about problems of ethnocentrism, rudeness and lack of concern for the individual, as well as racism.

One of the key issues in providing better care is to improve the communication skills of care givers. Poor communication has been a major cause of complaint for all patients since the beginning of research on patients' views of health care in the early 1960s (eg McIver, 1993b; Cartwright, 1964; Williams and Calnan, 1991).

In an article describing how nurses can be trained to develop culturally sensitive care, Lynam (1992) identifies four important elements in communicating with patients whatever their ethnic background. These are:

★   Create a dialogue with clients on care-related issues
★   Establish mutual understanding with clients
★   Identify a common goal in care
★   Establish a plan to work towards a common goal

She adds that the communication skills learned should include:

> ... *Responding empathically, validating clients, effectively summarising content and affective messages.*
>
> (Lynam, 1992)

An examination of what comprises good communication between health care professionals and patients can also be found in McIver (1993b).

A knowledge of why various minority ethnic groups have immigrated to the UK, the type of culture and society they left and the circumstances they now find themselves in, including inequalities in access to health care, will be very useful to health care providers. Details of different cultural practices, such as the religious observances of Muslims, Hindus, Buddhists etc, will also be useful. But care must be taken to avoid stereotyping individuals.

This kind of knowledge is only useful if it is used in conjunction with working practices that encourage the collection of details about religion, diet etc from every individual.

Unfortunately stereotyping people from the way they look, speak or behave is very common and if health care providers allow themselves to do it, they will not be able to provide appropriate care.

There is plenty of evidence that stereotyping occurs all too often in the NHS. For example, midwives in a study carried out by Bowler (1993) held stereotyped views of the 'thick' women from the large council estate. Some aspects of the 'working class' stereotypes (eg low intelligence, lack of compliance) were present in their stereotypes of Asian women; but Bowler adds:

> ... *This does not fully explain the extreme negative typification they suffered. The typifications go beyond class and echo the stereotypes of black and minority people common in wider society.*
>
> (Bowler, 1993, p. 158)

Bowler also found that when she recommended a book about caring for Muslims in response to a request for information, the midwife concerned said she didn't have time to read books. What she wanted was:

> ... *An A4 bit of paper with it all on so we can look things up when we need them.*
>
> (Bowler, 1993, p. 175)

As Bowler points out, this reaction assumes all 'Asians' are the same, and avoids the question of how care sensitive to the needs of individuals can be provided.

One way of avoiding stereotyping is to develop questioning skills and procedures. Some guidelines are provided by Baxter (1988) who makes a number of useful points. For example, a large proportion of the UK black population were born in the UK, so it is unwise to start off by asking a person about their country of origin.

Also it is best to be as concrete and specific as possible: it is better to ask 'What did you eat yesterday?', rather than 'What do you usually eat?'

Covering some topics adequately may take several questions. On religion, for example, it may be necessary to ask: 'Do you have a religion? Are you practising? Would you like to pray in hospital? What can we do to help?'

Advice on communicating with people who do not speak English is available (Henley, 1986, 1988; National Extension College, 1991); but this issue will be dealt with in greater detail below.

In sum, in order to provide culturally sensitive care health professionals need to understand the role of culture in an individual's life, particularly how it can affect their understanding and behaviour with respect to illness; and they need a knowledge of different cultures.

They also need to be aware of how economic and social structures reproduce stereotypical attitudes, racism and inequalities in health, and how organisations can prevent individuals from putting into practice the principles of culturally sensitive care.

They should develop good communication skills, and also practices to support and supplement these skills, such as questions or reminders in nursing records, and checklists.

Finally, they should understand that the principles involved in providing culturally sensitive care to black patients are similar to those involved in providing good care to all patients.

Having said this, there are four priority areas as far as black patients are concerned, and an examination of these areas makes it clear that enough research has already been carried out to show how changes to improve services can be carried out immediately.

Communication

In many studies of black people's views about health services, communication emerges as the most important issue.
For example:

> *The single most important factor which came out spontaneously,*
> *among respondents whose first language was not English, was the*
> *language barriers they faced when interacting with health and*
> *social care professionals ... many respondents were of the opinion*
> *that the lack of ability to adequately communicate with*
> *professionals and vice-versa was the only problem they had.*
>
> (Swarup, 1993, p. 41)

> *Access to local services is hindered by communication difficulties.*
> *30 per cent of local Asian people have difficulties communicating*
> *in English. The majority were female. Difficulties with*
> *understanding treatment and expressing symptoms is the major*
> *problem affecting local Asian people in gaining access to health*
> *services, particularly for outpatient attendances and inpatient*
> *admissions.*
>
> (Dumelow and Bailey, 1993, p. 37)

> *... The importance of communication is underlined by the fact*
> *that patients who spoke good English or had found a Chinese nurse*
> *on the ward were more likely to be satisfied than other patients.*
> *Several people commented on apparent misunderstandings and*
> *confusion about the purpose of the treatment they had received*
> *in hospital.*
>
> (Bloomsbury HA, 1984, p. 22)

Some studies provide quotes from respondents and these can illustrate the problem only too clearly. A Chinese women said:

> *I was in hospital for one week. I couldn't communicate with*
> *anyone. Although they tried to be helpful, I felt very alienated and*
> *isolated. I was scared.*
>
> (Swarup, 1991, p. 88)

Clearly those who cannot communicate are at a serious disadvantage. Among the reasons are:

★   Hospitals are frightening places at the best of times. Those who cannot understand what is being said have more difficulty understanding what is happening to them. They are likely to be more anxious and have no way of expressing that anxiety or getting reassurance.

★   They will be unable to explain symptoms properly and may receive a wrong diagnosis because of this.

★   They may not follow instructions because they do not understand them or can't understand the reason for them.

A study of acute psychiatric services at Parkside Health Authority (GPMH, 1992) commented that the mental health units do not make as much use of the interpreting service as other hospital departments. This led the researchers to ask:

> *How are people whose first language is not English assessed appropriately for compulsory admission?*
>
> (GPMH, 1992, p. 85)

Studies have shown that there is a disproportionate representation of some groups of black people in mental health services, whilst others are under-represented (Littlewood and Lipsedge, 1989). Also, members of some groups are more likely to be detained under the Mental Health Act than others.

A study by the Bethlem Royal and Maudsley Hospitals Special Health Authority (Caan, 1993) found that members of African, Caribbean and Indian ethnic minorities made up 27.5 per cent of patients detained under the Mental Health Act, compared with 9.5 per cent of patients who had not been sectioned.

Patients who had been sectioned were significantly less likely to understand why they had been admitted. These patients were also significantly less likely to think that the hospital was doing good for their health.

The Parkside study carried out by GPMH (1992) also found that only 51 per cent of people felt that their treatment had been discussed with them and that they had had a choice about it.

Many of the young black patients said they felt they had to try not to make trouble for themselves. This included not asking questions about their treatment, diagnosis and future, and accepting what they were told even if they did not agree with it.

This example highlights the fact that improving communication is not just about providing interpreters, but also about setting people at ease and explaining issues such as diagnosis and treatment carefully. This may have to be done on several occasions, because when people are ill or under stress they are not always able to absorb what is being said to them.

For many people, though, an interpreter is essential. There is a remarkable amount of prejudice directed at people who cannot speak English. Studies have shown that many health professionals feel black patients should know how to speak English and that if they don't they must be stupid.

The study carried out by Bowler (1993) is an eye-opener in this regard. Asked if the hospital was considering employing interpreters, one consultant answered:

> *Of course not. We haven't even got enough nurses. If you ask me they shouldn't be allowed into the country until they can pass an English exam.*
>
> (Bowler, 1993, p. 161)

This attitude is not uncommon and has been in existence for some time. Seven years ago Henley (1986) was commenting that:

> *Considering the drastic effects of the language barrier on patient care, remarkably little effort is made to ensure that non-English speakers can always or usually communicate with their health workers ... How many non-English speaking patients end up getting nothing but veterinary style physical care?*
>
> (Henley, 1986, p. 19)

As Henley notes, it is unreasonable to expect all black patients to know English. All adults find new languages difficult; many have also had no formal education and have no confidence in their ability to learn English. Most meet very few English speakers and encounter hostility or impatience when they do.

Those most affected seem to be elderly people, who may also experience diminished vision and hearing capacity (Darby, 1989; Stoyle, 1993); those from outside the new Commonwealth, such as Chinese, Vietnamese, Somali, Ethiopian, Turkish and Greek people; newly arrived refugees; and women from India and Pakistan, particularly Bengali speakers (Slater, 1993).

Clearly interpreting services are a necessity, and these can be made available by recruiting more bilingual staff, employing trained interpreters, making use of local interpreting agencies, or using telephone interpreting services such as Language Line.

Staff should be trained to use interpreters, and guidance on this can be found in Henley (1986, 1988) and National Extension College (1991). These publications also provide very useful guidance on how to communicate across a language barrier and generally set at ease those whose first language is not English. A *few* examples from these essential booklets are:

★ Speak slowly and clearly but do not raise your voice.

★ Choose words the patient is likely to know.

★ Use pictures or mime.

★ Think before you speak, and break the topic down into logical steps.

★ Signal when you change the subject.

★ Try to learn a few words of the patient's language, such as 'good morning', 'good night', 'yes', 'no'.

★ Keep a phrase book (it can cheer patients up to hear someone struggling to pronounce familiar words).

★ Use Red Cross language cards.

One little understood aspect highlighted in these and similar publications is the different ways in which names are constructed among black cultures. Nursing records should be designed to accommodate different naming systems, and some knowledge of the systems is clearly essential if names are to be recorded correctly. All patients should be asked how they wish to be addressed, whatever their ethnic origin.

Guidance on communicating with non-English speaking patients (eg Henley, 1986, 1988; National Extension College, 1991) is not meant as a substitute for interpreters, but a way of helping non-English speaking patients when interpreters aren't at hand.

It is also important to mention again that interpreters can only translate information. Their role is not to help patients to handle difficult situations or argue their own case, as advocates can; nor is it to help local communities understand what health services are available, improve access to them, and help service users to express their views about what might improve services, as linkworkers and other types of development workers are able to (see NAHA, 1988, for examples).

Information Provision

As one aspect of communication, information provision in the NHS has never been very good, and patients have complained about inadequacies in this area for many years (Jones, Leneman and MacLean, 1987).

Along with other types of service user, black people consider better information provision to be a high priority. The topic is brought up in every study. For example:

> *Nearly one-third (31 per cent) of all people surveyed said that more information was needed regarding the health service available.*

> (Swarup, 1993, p. 95)

> *... Many of the more settled respondents were of the opinion that no information was given to ethnic minority groups about the general activities of service provisions and about the specifics of what was available to them ... It was suggested that at present, people neither knew where to go for help or what was available.*

(Shah, Harvey and Coyle, 1993, p. 41)

> *Lack of information about services, about black and minority ethnic people, about legal structures within which services are provided and information targeted at black and minority ethnic people, were the most frequently mentioned problems affecting access to services. Leaflets, even where they are translated into community languages, are a relatively inefficient way of making information accessible.*

(Ogunsola, 1991, p. 72)

At present information provision in the NHS is patchy, but a recent overview of the area identified the following different types of information (McIver, 1993b):

★   What services are available

★   How best to use services

★   What will happen when using services

★   What standards of services to expect

★   How to stay healthy

★   About particular illnesses and diseases

★   About what happens during particular operations, tests and treatments

★   About self care after operations or following diagnosis

★   About the effects and side effects of drugs and treatments

★   About choices of treatment

Where this information is available it has rarely been developed *with* patients, and so may not cater to their needs. Even less often are versions appropriate to black patients developed.

In some areas this lack of information has very serious consequences. For example, informed consent is almost impossible because information about operations and consent forms are never available in alternative languages, and professional interpreters are rarely used.

People from black communities rarely make formal complaints, and this is probably because details of how to make a complaint are not often translated or widely publicised among these communities.

A survey of diabetes clinics with more than 50 Asian people on the register found that 40 per cent had no adapted diet sheets and 34 per cent had no hospital interpreter (Mello, 1992). It is not surprising to find that studies show that Asian patients with diabetes know less about their illness and have poorer glycaemic control than white diabetics (Hawthorne, 1990).

There are two main problems facing those wishing to develop good quality information for black people. First, translations are not always suitable; and secondly, many people may not read the language they speak.

Translations can be difficult and the unwary may find themselves with a translated leaflet which is full of errors. By using experienced translators, checking the information with health professionals who read the language and have experience of the information being given, and piloting the leaflet among potential readers, many problems can be avoided.

A booklet produced by North East Thames Regional Health Authority gives guidance on producing health information for non-English speaking people (NE Thames RHA, 1990).

However, sometimes concepts are difficult to translate, because no equivalent words are available, or because the whole body of information would be better set within a different cultural context. Then it is better to get someone to rewrite the whole leaflet in the appropriate language, and translate it into English only to check that the message is correct.

This procedure was adopted for a leaflet entitled 'Your Heart – How to Look After It', written in Bengali and published by the Bloomsbury Health Promotion Department and Bloomsbury Department of Nutrition and Diabetics.

The leaflet was written by a doctor from Bangladesh and a woman in the Bangladesh community who had heart problems. An Asian graphic designer took photographs of local families and included these in the text.

A community development health promotion officer involved in the production of the leaflet said the process had worked well, but that next time she would like to involve more people in the community to make sure that the information produced catered to their needs.

The development officer was critical of the type of leaflet in which the same information is translated into five Asian languages. She suggested trying to imagine producing a leaflet with the same information on diet and nutrition for English, French, Italian, German and Dutch readers. Since the diets vary it would be quite difficult (Ogunsola, 1993).

The Health Education Authority has co-ordinated the production of a wide range of health promotion materials for black people (see 'Useful Addresses').

As many black people do not read the language they speak, other ways of getting information to them will have to be organised.

Apart from using linkworkers and community development officers, other suggestions are to produce information on audio-cassette: for example, the Bloomsbury & Islington Health Promotion Department produce information on women's health, breast feeding and HIV prevention in Sylheti dialect. Video cassettes can also be used.

Cassettes can be made available through clinics, community centres, mosques and temples, day nurseries, play groups and schools, women's groups, GP surgeries, libraries, video shops and food shops catering to ethnic communities.

Diet

Although hospital food is quite high on the list of issues that white patients complain about, there is evidence that black patients are generally more dissatisfied about food than white patients.

For example, Ahmad (1990) found that more Asian than white patients did not eat hospital food and more gave the reason that they did not like the food (13 per cent compared to 1.3 per cent). Only 63 per cent of Asians in this study said they had sufficient choice of food, compared with 83 per cent of whites.

During an interview survey carried out to inform guidelines for the booklet *Health for All Our Children*, Slater (1993) found that only 48 per cent of children in the study ate the hospital food provided.

A survey of 30 young Afro-Caribbean womens' experiences and perceptions of pregnancy and childbirth (Larbie, 1985) found that the woman were unanimous in their criticism of hospital food. The majority ate a diet substantially different from the white population. Larbie writes:

> *Surprisingly, although twenty-three of the women were born in England, they stated they were unfamiliar with the English diet and its blandness and thought it was unhealthy.*

(Larbie, 1985, p. 25)

Unfortunately, despite the fact that the provision of culturally appropriate food would seem to be a fairly straightforward operation, there is evidence that in practice it is difficult to achieve.

For example, Shah, Harvey and Coyle (1993) found that although South Glamorgan Health Authority had a food and health policy for multi-cultural groups, respondents in the study were not offered culturally acceptable meals. Most of the respondents said either that they ate boiled vegetables in hospital, or that their family brought in food from home.
At another hospital, ethnic food was kept in stock in the freezers but was not included on the menu because there was said to be no demand for it (Hanley, 1993). This was clearly a circular position: without it being advertised on the menu, how were patients to know it was available?

It is not just a question of serving 'curries', vegetables or salads. The diets of different black groups vary a great deal and familiar food is important if a person is feeling ill. Not only do they need to eat in order to get proper nourishment so that they can recover, but food that is enjoyable also helps to make people feel better. Many white people are vegetarian or appreciate foreign food, so more variety would be of benefit to all patients.

In addition, food can be a religious issue for black patients, and they will need to be convinced that the proper procedures have been observed in its preparation. This means that the food will have to be approved by a religious leader who can inform the patient (eg by letter or certificate, or through community networks) that the food is OK to eat.

Details of what is and is not acceptable to different groups and under what circumstances they fast, together with checklists to help providers improve catering for black people can be found in Henley (1988) and the National Extension College (1991). See also Hill's book (1990) on catering for black tastes.

Religious and Cultural Needs

Religion is very important at critical points in the life cycle and at times of crisis, yet hospitals rarely provide places where non-Christians can go to pray and this can be a source of great embarrassment and distress to those concerned.

At the very least patients should be asked whether they wish to pray in hospital, whether they do this at set times, and whether they need to kneel on the floor, or if drawing curtains around the bed is sufficient.

The offer of the use of a clean side room or curtained area of a room will prevent patients going through an experience similar to that of one Muslim respondent in Swarup's (1992) study:

> *I feel too embarrassed to pray on the floor where everyone would give me strange looks.*
>
> (Swarup, 1993, p. 87)

Swarup found that the lack of prayer facilities in hospitals for people of faiths other than Christian was noted by several respondents.

Slater (1993) reported that for many of the families interviewed, practising their religion while in hospital was still important: 35 per cent wanted to pray while in hospital and 22 per cent wanted a religious leader of their faith to visit them in hospital.

Pegram (1988) comments that the section concerning religious observances on a patient's nursing assessment form is rarely completed, yet the Royal College of Nursing states that the content of a good care plan should include not only physical care but also spiritual requirements.

The Patient's Charter makes it clear that a patient's religious and cultural needs are important, so it is to be hoped that this section will be given proper attention in future.

For many patients religious observances involve more than prayer and spill over into other aspects of life, such as washing, hair and body care, family planning, birth and death, and whether certain medical procedures are allowed.

These areas of life are also likely to be influenced by different cultural traditions. Guidance on these issues can be found in Slater (1993), Henley (1988), National Extension College (1991).

Summary

It is important to start establishing mechanisms for collecting the views of black people about health services, but enough research has already been carried out to show how some improvements to services can be implemented immediately.

Many studies have shown that communication, information provision, diet, and religious and cultural needs are high on the list of areas where improvements are necessary.

These issues are covered by the Patient's Charter and are areas where improvements will be of benefit to all patients, not just those from black groups.

I   Health professionals need to devise ways of setting standards relating to these issues (an example is given in Pegram, 1988).

II They need to design nursing records and similar forms to collect information about language(s) spoken and read, diet and religion.

III They need to develop questioning and interviewing skills, and checklists to reinforce them, to deal with these issues sensitively and in sufficient detail (see eg Baxter, 1988).

IV Service standards in these areas should be monitored by asking black patients for their views and experiences of hospitals at discharge or shortly after their return home. Chapter 6 presents some examples of questions to ask about these issues.

6 EXAMPLES OF QUESTIONS TO ASK BLACK PATIENTS

There is no reason why black patients should not be asked the same questions about their views on services as other patients. Examples of questions to ask patients about different services areas are given in earlier publications in this series.

Having said this, it may be worth conducting a survey or study asking questions of particular relevance to black people, either alone or in combination with other questions. These questions can be given to a mixed sample of white patients and those from other ethnic groups in order to make comparisons, or to minority ethnic patients only.

Examples of questions to ask can be formulated from the research highlighting areas of concern for black and minority patients described in the previous chapter. Some suggestions are provided below, for patients using hospital services.

Those wishing to survey patients using these example questions should (i) bear in mind the advice given in Chapter 3 about methods, (ii) obtain advice on questionnaire construction if they do not themselves have this expertise, and (iii) pilot the questionnaire with a small sample of patients before wider use.

1   What languages do you speak?

....

....

2   How well do you speak English?

☐   Not at all
☐   Slightly
☐   Quite well
☐   Very well

3   When you were in hospital were you able to talk to those who cared for you?

☐   Not at all
☐   On some occasions
☐   Most of the time
☐   All of the time

Comments   ....

....

4   When you were in hospital were the staff able to understand your expressed needs?

☐   Yes
☐   No

Comments   ....

....

5   Was an interpreter available?

☐   I did not need one
☐   No, not at all
☐   On some occasions
☐   Most of the time
☐   Every time I needed one

6 Was the interpretation of a good standard?

☐ Yes, I was satisfied
☐ No, I was unhappy about it

If no, why was this? ....
....

7 What language(s) do you read (if any)?

....

8 Were you given any written information before you went into hospital about your visit?

☐ Yes
☐ No

9 Were you given any written information while you were in hospital (eg about your treatment)?

☐ Yes
☐ No

10 Have you read the information you were given?

☐ I did not get any
☐ Yes, I have read it
☐ No, I have not read it
☐ No, I cannot read it
☐ Someone has read it to me

11 Would you have liked further information about some aspect of your hospital visit, treatment and care etc?

☐ Yes
☐ No

If yes, please describe what you would have liked further information about ....
....

12 Do you know how to make a complaint should you need to?

☐ Yes
☐ No

Comments ....
....

13 Do you feel that your treatment and care was discussed adequately with you?

☐ Yes
☐ No

If no, please explain why you feel this ....
....

14 Are you happy with the treatment you received?

☐ Yes
☐ No

If no, please explain why not ....
....

15 If you were prescribed any medicines or tablets, have you taken them as instructed?

☐ Yes
☐ No
☐ I'm not sure

If no, please explain why not ....
....

16 Were you able to eat the hospital food?

☐ No, I had food brought in
☐ I ate some but I didn't like it
☐ Yes, it was OK
☐ Yes, it was excellent

17 Were you able to pray if you wanted to?

☐ I did not want to pray
☐ I wanted to pray but couldn't
☐ I was able to pray as I wanted

18 Do you feel your religious needs were satisfied?

☐ Yes
☐ No

If no, why was this? ....

....

19 Were you embarrassed at any time during your stay in hospital?

☐ Yes
☐ No

If yes, please describe the circumstances ....

....

20 Were there any ways in which your stay in hospital could have been made more pleasant for you?

....

....

7 CONCLUSIONS

Service development and research on issues affecting black people is often treated as special and kept separate from mainstream work.

Where research on 'patient satisfaction' is concerned this is completely unnecessary because not only do many of the same methods apply, whatever the ethnicity of the patient, but also the issues which emerge as of most importance to patients (improved communication, better information provision, appropriate treatment and care) occur across all ethnic groups.

Having said this, it should not be seen as an excuse for health professionals to ignore the fact that some methods are unsuitable or that methods that do work may require extra preparation to overcome language differences and lack of motivation.

Many white people are not interested in taking part in health surveys because they feel that their views will not make any difference. This is doubly so for black people who have found that despite previous research and 'special projects', services still do not seem to cater to their needs.

There is no doubt that black people find health services less easy to use than do white people. Similar problems occur for all patients, but for black service users they are more severe.

For example, many white patients find hospitals impersonal places where they are not always kept informed of what is happening to them. Sometimes they feel like a number rather than a person and wish someone had the time to answer their questions and explain things more fully. Many black people feel exactly the same, except that the situation is worse because they cannot understand what is being said at all. Replying to questions may be impossible, let alone asking them.

On top of feeling they are being treated as a number, they may also feel they are not getting as much attention as other patients and that their attempts to communicate are treated with dismissal. They may think staff see them as stupid and consider them to be creating a fuss about nothing because they are 'foreign'.

However well meaning health professionals may be, this is what patients have said in studies which get further than a superficial 'satisfied' response. The research described in Chapter 5 clearly shows that many black patients, although grateful to be treated when they are sick and vulnerable, often find their hospital experience an unpleasant one.

Exactly how many or what proportion of black patients feel this way and how this compares with white patients is difficult to say, because most of the research described has been of a qualitative nature. Sufficient qualitative research findings have been accumulated to justify making changes along the lines described in Chapter 5, but more than that is dependent upon further quantitative research.

Making improvements immediately will help to convince black people that their views count and will encourage them to take part in further research.

When routinely monitoring user views of service standards, health professionals should include questions relevant to black patients (see Chapter 6 for examples), make sure they are able to distinguish between the responses of different ethnic groups (see Chapter 4), and use a method which makes it possible for black patients to respond (see Chapter 3).

A combination of immediate improvements and appropriate consultation and routine monitoring should help all types of health professionals to develop 'culturally sensitive services', especially if they are also given opportunities to discover how different social and cultural experiences affect understanding of health and illness.

Health workers in both purchaser and provider organisations need to understand which methods are most appropriate for obtaining the views and experiences of black populations, as well as the ethical issues surrounding this research. The following lists summarise key activities in which each type of organisation should be engaged (see Gunaratnam, 1993, and Mohammed, 1993, for further details).

Providers should be:

★ Developing systems and procedures to monitor patterns of activity, indicators of health needs and outcomes of care by ethnicity.

★ Ensuring that complaints and suggestion procedures are accessible to and appropriate to black patients and carers and that they are well publicised within black communities.

★ Using appropriate methods to obtain the views and experiences of black patients and linking these initiatives to planning and decision-making processes.

★ Linking ethnic monitoring to service planning and review, and quality management systems.

Purchasers should be:

★ Ensuring that they have identified local black populations, and that their health needs assessment process includes measures to find out the needs of these populations.

★ Enabling black groups to take part in the commissioning process.

★ Ensuring that provider units have mechanisms for discovering the views and experiences of black patients and carers.

★ Ensuring that research on patients' views and ethnic monitoring informs service planning and delivery.

Those working in the NHS in whatever capacity should take such opportunities as are presented to them to discover how different social and cultural experiences affect understanding of health and illness.

Such knowledge is essential for developing culturally sensitive services, as is the motivation to treat the views of health service users as equal to those of health professionals.

USEFUL ADDRESSES

Association of Community Interpreters and Translators, Advocates and Linkworkers (ACITAL)
20 Compton Terrace
London N1 2UN
Tel: 071 359 6798

Commission for Racial Equality
Publications from:
Lavis Marketing
73 Lime Walk
Headington
Oxford OX3 7AD
Tel: 0865 67575

**Ethnic Minorities Health:
A Current Awareness Bulletin**
Medical Library
Field House Teaching Centre
Bradford Royal Infirmary
Bradford
West Yorkshire BD9 6RJ
Tel: 0274 364130

Health Education Authority
Hamilton House
Mabledon Place
London WC1H 9TX
Tel: 071 383 3833

Institute of Race Relations
2–6 Leeke Street
London WC1X 9HS

The Refugee Council
3 Bondway
London SW8 1SJ
Tel: 071 582 6922

Services for Health and Race Exchange (SHARE)
King's Fund Centre
126 Albert Street
London NW1 7NF
Tel: 071 267 6111

REFERENCES

Ahmad M. 'Inpatient satisfaction survey in Birch Hill Hospital, Rochdale.' *M Public Health Thesis*, University of Liverpool, 1990.

Atkin K. 'Community care in a multi-racial society: incorporating the user view.' *Policy and Politics*, 1991; 19 (3): 159–166.

Balarajan R, Soni Raleigh V. *Ethnicity and Health: A Guide for the NHS.* Department of Health, 1993.

Barr L, Rogers S. 'Evaluating health care services.' *Health Services Management*, 1991; February.

Baxter C. 'Culture shock.' *Nursing Times*, 1988; 84 (2), 13 January: 36–38.

Bloomsbury Community Services Unit/Bloomsbury Community Health Council. *The Health Care Needs of Chinese People in Bloomsbury Health District.* December, 1984.

Blumhagen D. 'Hyper-Tension: a folk illness with a medical name.' *Culture, Medicine and Psychiatry*, 1980; 4: 197–227.

Bowler I. '"They're not the same as us": Midwives' stereotypes of South Asian descent maternity patients.' *Sociology of Health and Illness*, 1993; 15 (2): 157–178.

Bowling A et al. *'Local Voices' in Purchasing Health Care. An Exploratory Exercise in Public Consultation on Priority Setting.* Needs Assessment Unit, Departments of Public Health and General Practice and Primary Care, St Bartholomew's Hospital Medical College, 1992.

Bowling A et al. *'Local Voices' in Purchasing Health Care.* King's Fund Centre, 1993.

Bradburn J et al. 'Community based cancer support groups: an undervalued resource?' *Clinical Oncology*, 1992; 4: 377–380.

Butt, J. 'More than just record keeping.' *SHARE Newsletter*, 1992; 2, March.

Caan W. *Satisfaction Survey of Special Health Authority Inpatients* (in progress). Bethlem Royal & Maudsley Hospitals Special Health Authority, 1993.

Calnan M. 'Towards a conceptual framework of lay evaluation of health care.' *Social Science Medicine*, 1988; 27 (9): 927–933.

Calvillo E R, Flaskerud J H. 'Evaluation of the pain response by Mexican American and Anglo American women and their nurses.' *Journal of Advanced Nursing*, 1993; 18: 451–459.

Camberwell CHC. *Visit to Dulwich Hospital, 4 December, 1992*. Camberwell CHC, 75 Denmark Hill, London SE5 8RS, 1992.

Carr-Hill R, McIver S, Dixon P. *The NHS and its Customers*. Centre for Health Economics, University of York, 1989.

Cartwright A. *Health Surveys in Practice and in Potential*. King Edward's Hospital Fund for London, 1983, 1988.

Cartwright A. *Human Relations and Hospital Care*. Routledge Kegan Paul, London, 1964.

Changing Health Services. *Report of a Conference Held on 8 October, 1992 in Camden & Islington to Meet the Needs of Black and Other Minority Ethnic Communities*. Camden Racial Equality Council, 58 Hampstead Road, London NW1 2PY.

Cohen F. 'Postsurgical pain relief. Patients' status and nurses' medication choices.' *Pain*, 1980; 9 (1): 265–274.

Cornwell J, Gordon P. *An Experiment in Advocacy. The Hackney Multi-Ethnic Women's Health Project*. King's Fund Centre, 1984.

Darby S. 'Culture club.' *Nursing the Elderly*, 1989; July: 20–21.

Davitz J, Davitz L. *Influences on Patients' Pain and Psychological Distress*. Springer-Verlag, New York, 1981.

Dixon P. *Some Issues in Measuring Patient Satisfaction*. CCUFLINK 3, Community Consultation and User Feedback Unit, MCS, Welsh Health Common Services Authority, 1993.

Dudley S, Holm K. 'Assessment of the pain experience in relation to selected nurse characteristics.' *Pain*, 1984; 18 (2): 179–186.

Dumelow C, Bailey J. *Uptake of Health Services by the Asian Community*. Directorate of Public Health Medicine, NW Surrey HA, 1993. From District Health Promotion Service, The White House, Crouch Oak Lane, Addlestone, Surrey KT15 2AN (Tel: 0932 854476). Copy in King's Fund Centre Library.

Dun, R. *Pictures of Health?* Health Rights/West Lambeth HA, 1989.

Goldmann A E, McDonald S S. *The Group Depth Interview: Principles and Practice.* Prentice-Hall, New Jersey, 1987.

GPMH. *Consumer Audit of Acute Psychiatric Services for Adults in Parkside Health Authority.* Good Practices in Mental Health, 1992.

Gunaratnam Y. *Checklist: Health and Race.* King's Fund Centre, 1993.

Hadlow J, Pitts M. 'The understanding of common health terms by doctors, nurses and patients.' *Social Science and Medicine*, 1991; 32 (2): 193–196.

Hanley R. Information given during discussion at Patient Representative Project Meeting, NAHAT, 1993.

Haringey HA. *Qualitative Needs Assessment Study of Somali and Eritrean Refugee Women in Haringey.* New River Health Authority Health Promotion, 1992.

Hawthorne K. 'Asian diabetics attending a British hospital clinic: a pilot study to evaluate their care.' *British Journal of General Practice*, 1990; 40: 243–247.

The Health and Race Project. 'Voluntary Health Organisations and Black Communities in Liverpool.' *ARVAC Bulletin*, 1990; 42.

Henley A. 'Nursing care in a multi-racial society.' *Senior Nurse*, 1986; 4 (2), February: 18–20.

Henley A. *Caring in a Multi-racial Society.* Bloomsbury Health Authority, Department of Community Medicine, 1988. Copy in the King's Fund Centre Library.

Hill S. *More Rice Than Peas: Guidelines to Improve Food Provision for Black and Ethnic Minorities in Britain.* Food Commission, 88 Old Street, London EC1V 9AR, 1990.

Holmes P. 'The patient's friend.' *Nursing Times*, 1991; 87 (19), 8 May: 16–17.

Jacox A. 'Assessing pain.' *American Journal of Nursing*, 1979; 79 (5): 894–900.

Jones L, Leneman L, MacLean U. *Consumer Feedback for the NHS: A Literature Review.* King Edward's Hospital Fund for London, 1987.

Joule N, Levenson R. *Effective Visiting for Community Health Councils.* Greater London Association of CHCs, 1992.

Jowell T, Larrier C, Lawrence R. *Joint CCSAP/King's Fund Centre Action Project into the Needs of Carers in Black and Minority Ethnic Communities in Birmingham,* 1990. Copy in the King's Fund Centre Library.

Kent A. 'Collecting ethnic group data in the NHS.' *SHARE Newsletter*, 1992; 2, March.

Koopman C, Eisenthal S, Stoeckle J D. 'Ethnicity in the reported pain, emotional distress and requests of medical outpatients.' *Social Science and Medicine*, 1984; 18: 487–490.

Krueger R A. *Focus Groups: A Practical Guide for Applied Research.* Sage
Publications, 1988.

Larbie J. *Black Women and the Maternity Services.* Health Education Council/
National Extension College for Training in Health and Race, 1985.

Leech K. *A Question in Dispute: The Debate About an 'Ethnic' Question in the
Census.* Runnymede Trust, 1989.

Lieber M. 'Patient representative is hospital–patient liaison.' *AORN Journal,*
1977; 2b (4), October: 668–674.

Lipton J, Marbach J. 'Ethnicity and the pain experience.' *Social Science and
Medicine,* 1984; 19: 1279–1298.

Littlewood, Lipsedge. *Aliens and Alienists: Ethnic Minorities and Psychiatry.*
Pelican, 1989.

Locker D, Dunt D. 'Theoretical and methodological issues in sociological
studies of consumer satisfaction with medical care.' *Social Science and Medicine,*
1978; 12: 283–292.

Lynam M J. 'Towards the goal of providing culturally sensitive care: principles
upon which to build nursing curricula.' *Journal of Advanced Nursing,* 1992; 17:
149–157.

MACHEM. *Manchester Action Committee on Health Care for Ethnic Minorities:
Annual Report 1990–91.* MACHEM, Room 20, Second Floor, Elliot House,
3 Jackson's Row, Off Deansgate, Manchester M2 5WD.

McIver S. *An Introduction to Obtaining the Views of Users of Health Services.*
King's Fund Centre, 1991.

McIver S. *Obtaining the Views of Inpatients and Users of Casualty Departments.*
King's Fund Centre, 1992.

McIver S. *Obtaining the Views of Users of Primary and Community Health Care
Services.* King's Fund Centre, 1993a.

McIver S. *Obtaining the Views of Users of Health Services about Quality of
Information.* King's Fund Centre, 1993b.

McIver S. *Investing in Patient's Representatives.* National Association of Health
Authorities and Trusts, 1993c.

McPherson B. 'Chinese lesson.' *Social Work Today,* 1992; 9 July: 19.

Mello M. 'Plugging the gap.' *Nursing Times,* 1992; 88 (3): October 21.

Mohammed S. *User-sensitive Purchasing.* King's Fund Centre, 1993.

Molzahn A, Northcott H. 'The social bases of discrepancies in health/illness
perceptions.' *Journal of Advanced Nursing,* 1989; 14: 132–140.

NAHA. *Action Not Words: A Strategy to Improve Health Services for Black and Minority Ethnic Groups*. National Association of Health Authorities, 1988.

National Extension College. *Caring for Everyone: Ensuring Standards of Care for Black and Ethnic Minority Patients*. The National Extension College Trust Ltd, 1991.

NE Thames RHA. *Health in Any Language – A Guide to Producing Health Information for Non-English Speaking People*. NE Thames RHA, Inhouse Public Relations, 40 Eastbourne Terrace, London, 1990.

NW/NE Thames RHAs. *Refugees in NW and NE Thames Regional Health Authorities*. NW & NE Thames RHAs, 1992.

Ogunsola A. *Equity and Access: Black and Minority Ethnic People's Health Project*. Research Report, 1991.

Ogunsola A. *The Department of Public Health Ethnic Monitoring Pilot Study (Consultant's Report)*. City and Hackney Health Authority, 1992. See also 'Ethnic Monitoring Trainers Pack'.

Ogunsola A. Personal communication, 1993.

Pearson M. 'The politics of ethnic minority health studies.' *Radical Community Medicine*, 1983; 16.

Pearson M. 'Racist notions of ethnicity and culture in health education.' In Rodnell S and Watt A (eds). *The Politics of Health Education*. RKP, 1986.

Pegram A. 'Extending awareness.' *Nursing Times*, 1988; 84 (27), 6 July.

Pollock A, Pfeffer N. 'Doors of perception.' *Health Service Journal*, 1993; 2 September.

Rankin M, Snider B. 'Nurses' perception of cancer patients' pain.' *Cancer Nursing*, 1984; 7 (2): 149–155.

Rashid A, Jagger C. 'Attitude to and perceived use of health care services among Asian and non-Asian patients in Leicester.' *British Journal of General Practice*, 1992; 42: 197–201.

Ravich R. *Where Have We Been?* A Review of the National Society of Patient Representatives and its Activities on the Occasion of the 10th Annual Meeting and Conference, 1981.

Rocheron Y, Dickinson R, Khan S. *Evaluation of the Asian Mother and Baby Campaign: A Synopsis*. Centre for Mass Communication Research, University of Leicester, 1989.

Ruddy B. 'Any port in a storm.' *Health Service Journal*, 1992; 26 November.

Sax A. 'Patient relations in risk management.' *Quality Review Bulletin*, 1979; April: 14–15.

Shah L, Harvey I, Coyle E. *The Health and Social Care Needs of Ethnic Minorities in South Glamorgan. Phase 1. A Qualitative Study.* Centre for Applied Public Health Medicine, University of Wales College of Medicine, 1993.

Sheldon T, Parker H. 'The Racialisation of Health Research.' Paper given at *BSA Annual Conference 'Health & Society'*, Manchester, March, 1991.

Shropshire HA/University of Birmingham. *Getting to the Core. A Practical Guide to Understanding Users' Experience in the Health Service.* Shropshire HA, Voss House, Shrewsbury SY5 6JN, 1992.

Silvera M. *Public Accountability: Black and Minority Ethnic Communities. Report of the First Stage of a Consultation Exercise with Voluntary Agencies and Community Groups.* Parkside Health Authority, 1992.

Sivanandan A. 'RAT and the degradation of black struggle.' *Race and Class*, 1985; 26 (4). Institute of Race Relations.

Slater, M. *Health for All Our Children: Achieving Appropriate Health Care for Black and Minority Ethnic Children and their Families.* Action for Sick Children, NAWCH, Argyle House, 29–31 Euston Road, London NW1 2SD, 1993.

Smith C H, Armstrong D. 'Comparison of criteria derived by government and patients for evaluating general practitioner services.' *British Medical Journal*, 1989; 299: 494–496.

SMSR (Social and Market Survey Research Ltd). *Ethnic Minority Healthcare In and Around Dewsbury.* Social and Market Survey Research Ltd, 82 Beverley Road, Hull HU3 1YD (Tel: 0482 211200), 1992. Copy in King's Fund Centre Library.

Speigal D, Bloom Y, Yalom I. 'Group support for patients with metastatic cancer: a randomised prospective outcome study.' *Archives of General Psychiatry*, 1981; 38: 527–533.

Stoyle J. *Caring for Older People: A Multi-cultural Approach.* Stanley Thornes Publishers Ltd, Cheltenham, 1991, 1993.

Swarup N. *Equal Voice: Black Communities' Views on Housing, Health and Social Services.* Report No. 22, Social Services Research and Information Unit, Portsmouth Polytechnic, Mill Dam, Burnaby Road, Portsmouth PO1 3AS, 1993. Copy in King's Fund Centre Library.

Teske K, Daut R, Cleeland C. 'Relationships between nurses' observations and patients' self-reports of pain.' *Pain*, 1983; 16 (3): 286–296.

Thomas V J, Rose F D. 'Ethnic differences in the experience of pain.' *Social Science and Medicine*, 1991; 31 (9): 1063–1066.

Thorogood N. 'Afro-Caribbean women's experience of the health service.' *New Community*, 1989; 15 (3): 319–334.

Thorogood N. 'Private medicine: "You pay your money and you gets your treatment!"' *Sociology of Health and Illness*, 1992; 14 (1): 23–38.

Walker R (ed). *Applied Qualitative Research*. Gower, London, 1985.

Williams S J, Calnan M. 'Convergance and divergence. Assessing criteria of consumer satisfaction across general practice dental and hospital care settings.' *Social Science and Medicine*, 1991; 33 (b): 706–716.

Zborowski M. 'Cultural components in response to pain.' *Journal of Social Issues*, 1952; 8: 16–30.